A Self-Care Guide for Leaders in Higher Education

A Self-Care Guide for Leaders in Higher Education

Building Your Plan for Professional Sustainability

Gretchen Oltman and Vicki Bautista

Teachers College Press
Teachers College, Columbia University

Published by Teachers College Press,® 1234 Amsterdam Avenue, New York, NY 10027

Front cover design by Holly Grundon / BHG Graphics.

Library of Congress Cataloging-in-Publication Data is available at loc.gov

ISBN 978-0-8077-8770-0 (paper)
ISBN 978-0-8077-8771-7 (hardcover)
ISBN 978-0-8077-8340-5 (ebook)

Printed on acid-free paper
Manufactured in the United States of America

Contents

Acknowledgments

Our gratitude extends to all of the professionals in higher education who have shared their stories with us. Your work is important and serves as the heartbeat of your campus. We appreciate your honest reflections of your lived experiences, your dedication to your students and campuses, and your willingness to devote your careers to the important calling of working for and with students in higher education. If we leave you with one message it is this: Take care of yourself in the midst of the changes and chaos that surrounds you. Prioritize what is important to you, live valiantly, and enjoy each day and consider how your actions impact your professional sustainability.

CHAPTER 1

You Matter

WHY YOU NEED A SELF-CARE PLAN FOR YOUR PROFESSIONAL SUSTAINABILITY

As the world changes around us, the demands on higher education professionals have steadily transformed to develop new enrollment and retention strategies, support student needs, incorporate new technology on campus, and provide opportunities for students to be workforce ready. Much of the focus working in any higher education institution is on serving other people—students, colleagues, community members—and often with attention on others. As a result, our own personal growth and care are often neglected. Yet securing and keeping experienced, knowledgeable professionals is an asset to higher education—they provide stability during change, a wealth of historical institutional knowledge, and professional wisdom that is difficult to duplicate. While tackling these challenges head-on may seem within the role of one's expected career focus, it is imperative for those in higher education to also consider their health and well-being by focusing on self-care if we hope to build sustaining and meaningful long-term careers within the higher education landscape.

It is apparent based on data from the 2023–2024 Healthy Minds Faculty and Staff Survey (HMS), which explores mental health and related topics for college faculty and staff, that well-being and self-care are not a priority when 57% of faculty reported "feeling burned out because of work" (Healthy Minds Network, 2024, p. 5). The survey defined burnout as "a state of prolonged physical and psychological exhaustion due to a person's work" (p. 5). On a positive note, 60% of respondents reported that they perceive their institution considers faculty and staff mental and emotional health a priority (p. 9).

There are a multitude of reasons why working in higher education is a preferred career-choice field, such as academic atmosphere, sense of community, relationships with colleagues, administrative support, students, and academic leadership (Mudrak et al., 2018). Furthermore, research focusing on faculty workplace engagement found the social climate, job autonomy, supportive supervision, position variety, ability to focus on innovation, and personal development opportunities were reasons that an academic career was fulfilling.

On the opposite side, research has demonstrated that stress associated with working in higher education centers around rising levels of work demands, job insecurity, and work–life balance conflicts (Mudrak et al., 2018). Working in higher education, at any level, either faculty or staff, presents challenges and obstacles that are faced in any long-term career path: intellectual exhaustion, frustration with leadership, confusion over strategic goals, and disappointment with lack of what was perceived to be a vibrant professional future.

SELF-CARE

While the term self-care is used frequently in everyday conversations on higher education campuses, there is not a consensus on the definition of self-care specific to higher education. As we spent time exploring the literature researching self-care in this realm, we were unable to find a theory, model, or definition that resonated with our vision for creating a self-care guide for higher education professionals. As a result, we began searching in other career fields to find a suitable definition for self-care. That is when we identified a concept analysis completed by Martínez et al. (2021) to investigate the characteristics that reflected the most frequently used terms associated with the concept of self-care. The results of the literature review established an operational definition outlining the concept and its defining attributes. The research team defined self-care as "the ability to care for oneself through awareness, self-control, and self-reliance in order to achieve, maintain, or promote optimal health and well-being" (p. 422). The first attribute, awareness, is the ability to recognize, evaluate, or be mindful of your health and well-being. The next attribute, self-control, is engaging in regulation and control of emotions. The last attribute, self-reliance, is using your own resilience, motivation, or resources to choose a course of action to achieve what you want (Martínez et al., 2021).

Self-care in higher education is not a linear path. It ebbs and flows based on the time of the academic year. Generally, the ramp-up to the fall term is full of planning for the new school year; once the term starts, there is a spike in adrenaline as all the details come together (or don't!). Then there is a month or so of steady routines until fall break. Once everyone returns, there is a steady uptick of work as the end of the term is in sight. After Thanksgiving, the steady uptick turns into a mad dash to the finish line, with final projects and exams, administrative tasks, and planning for the spring term. As winter break arrives, most are exhausted and ready for some rest and relaxation, but the unfinished details for the spring semester seem to linger, keeping you from fully enjoying the time away from work.

Similar to the fall semester, there is a spike in adrenaline as finishing touches are put on course syllabi, student activities are planned, and all the administrative tasks necessary to make the university run like a well-oiled machine are completed. Then there is a stretch of steady routines until spring break arrives. Once everyone returns, the thought of summer clouds the numerous things that must be completed—final projects and exams, graduation planning, and administrative responsibilities that need to be completed to wrap up the academic year, while planning for both the summer and fall semesters.

In the midst of the academic year, the busy parts and the repetitive everyday routines, it is important to anticipate what you can do to support your self-care and consider what small actions you can take each day to support your overall health and well-being. While cliché, it is true—you can't pour from an empty cup, and you need to place your own air mask on first before you can support the hustle and bustle of a busy college or university campus.

PROFESSIONAL SUSTAINABILITY

Being a successful higher education professional takes stamina, and successful individuals can only sustain their momentum for as long as they maintain their well-being. The Australian Council of Professions (2025) defines a "profession" as a disciplined group of individuals who adhere to ethical standards and are accepted by the public as possessing special knowledge and skills in a widely recognized body of learning derived from research, education and training at a high level, and who are prepared to apply this knowledge and exercise these skills in the interest of others (para. 1). A professional is generally regarded as someone who demonstrates certain traits that reflect competence, respect, and integrity in their work and interactions. Sustainability, on the other hand, is the quality of being able to continue something for a long period of time (Cambridge Dictionary, n.d.).

Former professor Elizabeth Haswell described the wide range of roles that faculty (and, really, any professional in higher education) serve, from teacher, to graphic designer, to public speaker, to mentor, to mental health monitor. She wrote, "For the most part, we are eager to work in these different capacities, and many of them are intrinsic to successful research careers. I can say from personal experience that stretching one's skill set can be enormously invigorating. However, as we take on new duties without removing old ones, our time and attention—which are not infinite—are being split into smaller and smaller pieces" (Haswell, 2017, para. 1). She argued that this continuous professional pulling causes a great deal of stress on today's faculty, as the culture of nonstop work, faster turnarounds, and drive for individual success is actually detrimental to the need for professionals to have time for meaningful reflection, critical thinking, and simply time for mental rest.

Considering these definitions, professional sustainability is the ability to consistently demonstrate competence, investment, and integrity in a profession for an extended period of time while maintaining a sense of balance and well-being. In other words, it's the ability to have space to be good at what you do, to be relied on to do your work well, to treat others with respect, and to maintain personal well-being while doing your job over a long period of time, despite increasing demands for productivity.

Professional sustainability is the ability to consistently demonstrate competence, investment, and integrity in a profession for an extended period of time while maintaining a sense of balance and well-being.

A VISION FOR SELF-CARE AND PROFESSIONAL SUSTAINABILITY

The combination of self-care and professional sustainability is typically considered in isolation, yet we encourage you to look at these two as complementary to each other and necessary for you to exist. Think about your self-care and professional sustainability like the far-away sunset in the image in Figure 1.1. You are in motion, living and working as you journey down the highway. Ahead of you is a landscape full of turns in the road and steep mountains—these are the obstacles and challenges that you will naturally face

Figure 1.1. Vision for Self-Care and Sustainability

Source: Reprinted with permission from Alexandra Laing.

in any profession. However, you also see the promise of the bright sun ahead—a point of career fulfillment and a destination that, when you arrive, will provide warmth and satisfaction. This visual can be a meaningful way to think about these two concepts in concert—the care we take to travel safely along this career journey and the promise of a professional impact that matters to you and to others.

WHY PROFESSIONAL SUSTAINABILITY CAN BE CHALLENGING

As higher education consistently changes to meet the needs of students, faculty, staff, and accrediting bodies, decisions have to be made related to these changes—how, when, and who will manage them. As we continually manage these changes and the many decisions that guide the ongoing change, we may face a phenomenon referred to as decision fatigue. The concept of decision fatigue was introduced by psychologist Roy F. Baumeister, who researched people's decision-making capabilities (Baumeister et al., 2007). He found that a person's ability to make decisions became worse after making many decisions, as their brain became fatigued. An analogy shared by Medical News Today compared the human brain to a battery, stating that "[e]ach decision reduces the charge of the battery, and the person has less energy available to make other decisions later" (Johnson, 2020, para. 7). In essence, the more decisions a higher education professional makes in a day, the more depleted they become. Wansink and Sobal (2007) found that we make approximately 221 decisions each day on food alone. As you consider the number of decisions that you make each day in both a personal and professional capacity, it is important to determine where you can create space to prioritize and create meaning in where you choose to spend your time. This is why it is important to create a plan to guide your self-care and enhance your professional sustainability. When you have an established plan, it decreases the decisions you need to make on a daily basis. As you read though the book, our hope is that we can bring attention to areas that may need some fine-tuning to reduce decision fatigue to enhance your well-being and professional sustainability.

ARE YOU A LEADER?

You are a leader. For the purposes of this book, we embrace a wide definition of leadership regardless of the title of position you hold. Within each chapter of this book, you'll read a synopsis of an area that impacts how we care for ourselves (or not) while working in higher education. We have not limited the audience of this book to deans, professors, or executives, but rather leaders in higher education. In this, we use a very wide approach to leadership—one that embraces the notion that every person working in any role on a campus is a leader. Our mantra, "Everyone is a leader," is drawn from leadership scholar Chris Lowney's statement in his book *Heroic Leadership*, where he noted, "Everyone is a leader, and everyone is leading all the time—sometimes in immediate, dramatic, and obvious ways, more often in subtle, hard-to-measure ways, but leading nonetheless" (Lowney, 2003, p. 17). In any role, you are making decisions, taking action, and contributing to the overall good of the institution—thus, your leadership matters.

Every campus relies on the participation of many in order to function—from the IT department ensuring secure access to campus resources, to the custodian cleaning a student study area, to the student worker answering a desk phone in the library. Each one of these individuals, at some point in time, is representing the institution as a whole, so we rely on their roles to contribute to the mission of the institution the same as we do a dean or provost. Anyone working in higher education can benefit from this book.

WHY WE WROTE THIS BOOK

We wrote this book because we have had the opportunity to interact with higher education professionals from around the world. We often speak on topics such as leadership, self-awareness, burnout, self-care, and well-being. The common theme that arose in the question-and-answer portion of the presentations or hallway conversations was that a lot of higher education professionals are struggling in the area of self-care. To be honest, we struggle in this area—often. As we explored the availability of resources for faculty and staff in higher education that provided guidance and support, the list was very short. So, we decided that was a sign we needed to write a self-care book for higher education professionals that focused on topics relevant to the career field and supported professional sustainability.

This book is written in a format to support your overall well-being in a way that is authentic to higher education professionals. You've heard, and probably tried, all of the usual self-care advice about exercising, eating better, sleeping more, being more mindful or, finding a hobby. While all of these ideas are beneficial, researched, and evidence based, is there still something that is keeping you from really finding enjoyment in your position? This book aims to help you identify the root cause of issues that impact your well-being so you can achieve professional sustainability in higher education.

This book is for all of our higher education colleagues who started in the career field because you were enthusiastic about sharing your knowledge and experiences with students; eager to support students in their exploration of new ideas, concepts, and professional opportunities; determined to support students in reaching their educational goals; and passionate about being part of something bigger than yourself. But somewhere along the way to supporting students and managing the ever-changing landscape of higher education you have become overwhelmed, exhausted, tired, stressed out, and burned out. Next, we will share our personal reasons for writing this book.

Vicki's Reason

My journey to working in higher education has been unique. I started my career in a variety of community and workplace wellness settings, including nonprofit, medical, government, and research. My journey to becoming a program director and faculty member in higher education unfolded as my career in community and workplace wellness provided opportunities to spend time in the higher education classroom, first as a guest lecturer, then as an adjunct. Engaging and collaborating with both undergraduate and graduate students sparked a sense of excitement, passion, and purpose. These teaching experiences solidified my desire to be in the higher education classroom full-time. While working in a staff role in higher education, I completed a doctoral program in interdisciplinary leadership. As luck would have it, a new bachelor's and master's program focusing on health and wellness was developed at the university I was employed at. Having a background in health and wellness and the educational credentials, I secured my first faculty role. Having the rare opportunity to work in higher education as both a staff member and faculty member, I hope to carry that perspective throughout the book. With over 15 years of higher education experience and leaning into my health coaching training, through this book I hope to empower others in the field to create a realistic and sustainable self-care plan that promotes professional sustainability.

Gretchen's Reason

I've spent most of my adult life in higher education in one form or another. For about the past 15 years I've worked at either a college or university and before that was a student for many, many years. In fact, I began my first college degree 35 years ago and, in that time, have always been connected to higher education either as a student or working professional. I am trained and have worked as a high school educator—a field known for burnout and, most recently, a massive exodus due to working conditions. I am also trained as an attorney, a field which, over time, has provided me the opportunity to witness some of my former law school classmates struggle with addictions, self-harm, and extremely detrimental work–life balance situations.

As a professional who has worked in several roles in higher education—from executive director to tenured associate professor—I have seen similar trends of burnout, personal dissatisfaction, and institutional abuse that have caused some of the smartest and most talented individuals to leave academia. To me, this weakens our plight as we seek to build institutions that are known as beacons of wisdom and academic freedom. With every colleague I've seen walk away from the profession, I've noticed that many of their departures could have been prevented had we paid better attention to the individual. Many have left because they received little to no recognition for long, arduous working hours, while others have moved to different professional roles that provided more money, better work–life balance, and recognition for their accomplishments rather than their deficits. In all of this, I hold hope for the state of higher education and feel that if we strategically acknowledge and address the assumptions that are made about how to best care for us as individuals and colleagues, we can help our institutions, and their people, adapt to doing so. But we have to lead this process, not stand aside and hope for the best.

DEFINITION OF TERMS USED THROUGHOUT THIS BOOK

To ensure consistency in language, ideas, and concepts throughout the book, the following section provides clear definitions of the key terms that will be used.

Burnout: A syndrome conceptualized as resulting from chronic workplace stress that has not been successfully managed. It is characterized by three dimensions: (1) feelings of energy depletion or exhaustion; (2) increased mental distance from one's job, or feelings of negativity or cynicism related to one's job; and (3) reduced professional efficacy, or not thinking you are successful in your role (World Health Organization, 2019).

Professional sustainability: The ability to consistently demonstrate competence, reliability, and respect in a profession for an extended period of time while maintaining one's own well-being.

Self-care: According to Martínez et al. (2021), this is "the ability to care for oneself through awareness, self-control, and self-reliance in order to achieve, maintain, or promote optimal health and well-being" (para. 37).

Stress: As defined by the World Health Organization (2023), it is "a state of worry or mental tension caused by a difficult situation. Stress is a natural human response that prompts us to address challenges and threats in our lives. Everyone experiences stress to some degree. The way we respond to stress, however, makes a big difference to our overall well-being" (para. 1).

Well-being: According to the Inter-Association Well-Being Collaborative, a collaboration of over 20 higher education associations, well-being is described as an optimal and dynamic state that allows people to achieve their full potential. The workgroup identified two interdependent types of well-being in higher education: individual and community. Individual well-being is defined within three broad and interrelated categories: (1) the perceived assessment of one's own life as being generally happy and satisfying, (2) having one's human rights and needs met, and (3) one's contribution to the community. Community well-being is defined by relationships and connectedness, perceived quality of life for all people in the community, and how well the community meets the needs of all members (NIRSA, 2020).

HOW TO USE THIS BOOK

This book will guide you through eight chapters introducing you to topics in higher education that directly impact our self-care and professional sustainability. These chapters will provide you with background information on the topic, engaging activities to explore the topic in greater depth, and reflective questions to further expand your thoughts on the topic presented. These chapters will address the following:

- Communication complexities
- Role clarity
- Lack of control
- The need for meaningful recognition
- Lack of confidence in leadership
- Delegation and trusting others
- Professional growth needs
- "Job creep" and high-achieving professionals

The final chapter will assist you in building a self-care plan for professional sustainability.

Within each chapter, you'll find relevant and timely information about how and why these topics show up in higher education as well as how and why each topic impacts our self-care and professional sustainability. These discussions lead to an engaging activity surrounding what you've learned. Last, a series of reflection questions prompts you to engage in further critical thinking, introspection, and engagement with each topic while you are in your daily routine.

CONCLUSION

Be ready to see yourself within the pages of this book. As you work your way through this book—and we do not anticipate that it will always be in a linear or straightforward fashion—we invite you to learn about each of the areas that has risen as critical to protecting, maintaining, and promoting self-care within higher education. We have built this book around our interactions with higher education professionals, from community college interns, to graduate student workers, to college presidents, through a series of self-care and burnout presentations and publications that we authored throughout the years. The topics within this book are the topics that resonated with our audiences—those that made their heads nod in ardent agreement or that brought out stories from their own campuses where self-care was ignored or outright detrimental to one's professional growth.

To begin the process of building a self-care plan for professional sustainability in higher education for yourself, it is important to explore your why. Reflect on the following questions thoughtfully and consider not only your history in higher education but also the current condition of your professional being:

- Why did you initially choose a career in higher education?
- Do you feel motivated to continue your work in higher education? Why or why not?
- Why have you chosen to stay in this profession rather than explore other career paths?
- Do you value the relationships you've built with colleagues and students in higher education? Why or why not?
- Do you believe that the work you do in higher education is worthwhile in the long run? Why or why not?

The answers to these questions will be important to return to as we explore different strategies to support your well-being and to build an individual self-care plan to hopefully be able to stay in the profession for many years to come.

CHAPTER 2

Communication Complexities

WHY DO WE STRUGGLE WITH COMMUNICATION IN HIGHER EDUCATION?

Leaders in higher education are held to a high standard of communicating not only well but with near perfection. Stanford professor Frances Quinn wrote, "More than just about any other leadership skill, people are fiercely criticized for poor communication. . . . The higher up you get, the more brutal that criticism becomes" (Moody, 2024, para. 2). In the 2024 Competencies for the College Presidency, the results of a survey of over 700 college presidents, being "communication savvy," or having the ability to communicate "effectively and authentically in formal and informal settings," was seen as a key attribute necessary for leading in today's colleges (Burmicky et al., 2024, p. 6). This included the need to effectively promote an institution's vision and value. The type of communication most sought after in today's settings included storytelling, personal messages that go past stock language or traditional institutional messaging, and messages that adequately reach diverse audiences. Survey respondents placed an emphasis on college leaders being able to articulate the "why" to their decisions in a personal and meaningful way, not just the "how."

We need communication skills (and processes) to be strong in higher education to function efficiently. There are enough political pressures, challenges to existing structures, and interpersonal disagreements happening that if we fail to prioritize how we are communicating, things can erode quickly. You might find yourself disengaging from difficult conversations because you know change is impossible, or you might escalate your voice because you feel unheard.

WHEN AND WHERE DID YOU LEARN TO COMMUNICATE?

It might be interesting to think about where and when you learned to communicate. This prompt might lead you back to your infancy or toddlerhood when you learned to speak or have a conversation, but think about that a bit deeper. When and where did you learn to really get a point across or convince someone that your way of thinking was the best? You've certainly changed and matured how you communicate during your career. Over time, you've probably had experiences on campus of both very good and very bad communication interactions. These stay in our minds because we are often surprised when conflict occurs or when what we think is being communicated clearly did not come out the way we intended.

Most of us learn to communicate in our roles through experience. That is, we learn from our lived interactions with others. As we've worked through various roles professionally, we've learned to tailor our approach—to be kinder when bad news is delivered or stronger when an appeal is desperately needed. We learn to choose our words wisely, and we more thoughtfully consider how to reach the audience with whom we are working. A presentation to the board of trustees is prepared differently than a check-in with an absent student, and we are expected to move between these roles easily.

OUR EXPECTATIONS FOR PERFECTION ARE CREATED THROUGH EXPERIENCES

The issue with communication in higher education really arises when the communication is not clear, is unpredictable, or does not consider the intended audience. Because of this, we end up making bad decisions based on faulty information, or we live in a constant state of unknown because we are just not sure where to get reliable information. This, then, causes us to question our own judgment and wonder if we really know what we are doing. Additionally, it can cause us to engage in practices that directly contradict meaningful dialogue and relationship-building including:

- **Learning and leaning on information gained through unofficial channels instead of from leadership directly:** This might be hearing about the resignation of a long-time colleague from your students or hearing that a new degree program is starting even though you didn't know there was a need for one. Without a clear path of where and when official communication (even unofficial, informal communication) should be coming from, the spouts are open and information pours from a variety of sources—some accurate, some highly unreliable.

- **Making decisions using outdated or erroneous information:** This happens when we continue doing the same practices over and over even though we've collected or learned new information that might change how we work. This is easy to do in higher education because we are doing a lot, year after year, and the processes become engrained in our day-to-day operations. There is rarely time to step back, examine a process, and revise missteps without causing disruption to the student or faculty experience.
- **Evaluation processes that are "in name" only:** If staff and faculty recognize that employee evaluation processes only impact the very worst employees (as a means of getting rid of them), a type of complacency sets in to where employees know their evaluation is essentially meaningless or has little impact on their job. This, in turn, builds employee dissatisfaction and disengagement. Thinking (or knowing) your annual evaluation is simply to check off a required box from HR creates a likelihood of less meaningful engagement or opportunity for professional growth. Yes, it keeps everyone at peace for a moment, but in the long run, bad employees learn to work the system to keep their jobs and good employees are disincentivized from participating in what is supposed to be a meaningful process.
- **Lack of understanding of the processes:** If communication falters and is unclear, wrong, or misunderstood, we are placed in a precarious position of having to assume things—how to complete a task, who needs what information, or when messaging needs to be tailored for a specific audience. This prevalence of assumptions can lead to further confusion about how communications are to be handled and by whom.
- **Challenges securing support for innovation, tangible items, or needs:** If we admit that we use communication as a tool to convince others of our plight—whether it be new laboratory space or additional faculty lines—we also

> must recognize the art of persuasion. If a need is not clearly supported with facts or anecdotal information, it can easily be dismissed as a desire or preference rather than a need.

Navigating unclear communication routes can be an untenable task in any higher education setting, and yet it hits us in a very personal way. Communication is at the core of everything that we do as a member of a campus community and yet the problem seems to be universal. Moreover, in recent times, communication avenues have multiplied, and expectations of near-perfect messaging are weighty. We cannot avoid communication, nor can we take the weight of that responsibility lightly. Yet when faced with the demands of communicating from frequency, mode, messaging, and audience, we also step into self-protection mode, seeking to communicate in ways that promote collegiality, trust, and transparency. We want to be known as someone who is good at communicating, yet we are sometimes fighting an influx of information that erodes trust in our work.

Let us not forget that the avenues we use to communicate have multiplied substantially to include social media, texting via personal devices, shared group messaging platforms, email, and face-to-face opportunities (among others). It is not atypical to spend hours online responding to student emails, faculty inquiries, and requests from administrators. Communication, whether explicitly outlined as such, is at the core of every job. Yet challenges with communication arise not only because of the many ways we are able to communicate but an additional need for precision, if not perfection.

CONSTANT CONTACT IN HIGHER EDUCATION

It may seem that constant attention to communication issues is built on some sort of obsession or compulsion for perfection. After all, if everyone communicates every single day, why is the world so critical of campus leaders? And how do we manage this call for personal, yet perfect communication while also maintaining our human capacity for making mistakes and missteps? And how do we know when we've communicated enough or not enough?

Stanford researchers Flynn and Lind (2023) suggest that leaders miscalibrate how much they are communicating. That is, if we are overestimating the amount we are communicating with colleagues yet they believe we are under-communicating, there is a disconnect in communication that is perceived as lacking in empathy. If this is the case, we are left guessing whether we are overwhelming our colleagues with too much information when less would suffice or creating divide when we don't provide as much information as desired.

If you've ever erroneously clicked "send" on an email, you recognize the feeling of dread of an unfinished or ill-timed message. You move into overdrive to cover your actions—from apologizing to sending a follow-up message clarifying or completing what you were attempting to convey. Sometimes this goes well, sometimes it does not. The same is true for interpersonal conversations or large group messaging—regardless of how many times you proofread or how a message appears to be conveyed from your perspective, there is always a risk of a misunderstanding. It is this risk that keeps us on edge and always in a cautionary mode. It is also this risk that keeps us at an arms-length distance from using communication to become more approachable and authentic.

In addition to how much or how little to communicate, we are also challenged with a need for heightened sensitivity to what is shared and with whom. Federal regulations like the Family Educational Rights and Privacy Act (FERPA) or institutional policies can limit the amount of information we are able to share with campus partners. Again, this lack of sharing can be perceived as hiding information when it is simply information that cannot legally or ethically be shared. This, in turn, creates a perception that cannot be avoided.

If the demand in today's higher education landscape is for personal and trustworthy messaging, so, too, is the need to vet for accuracy, inclusiveness, and timeliness. A heartfelt condolence sent on stock university stationery is less likely to be received as meaning well. A social media post congratulating a faculty member's achievement might be taken as a slight if similar accolades are not offered campus-wide for similar accomplishments. In all, on a human level, the compelling need for timeliness, perfection, and consistency can be overwhelming and can cause some to reduce communications to a minimalist approach for fear of offending someone or appearing less personal than desired by the recipients.

All of this—from considering what to share, how much to share, when to share, and with whom to share information—can cause internal and external stress within an already tenuous situation. A leader constantly on edge about saying the wrong thing or missing a point within communication will inevitably face scrutiny—warranted or not—that can cause personal distress.

HOW COMMUNICATION IMPACTS OUR SELF-CARE AND PROFESSIONAL SUSTAINABILITY

Being informed is a professional capacity at any career level. It provides a seat of knowledge, necessary information to work, and insights about an institution that help a person create a career of meaning and purpose. When communication fails—whether that be at the local level or at the institutional level—a sense of distrust can build. This distrust is tested as new information is shared (or not), and over time, one begins to determine the trustworthiness of the individuals sharing information and the institution as a whole.

In relationships, lack of communication leads to unclear expectations, feeling confused or lonely, or growing insecurity (Ryder, 2021). These same feelings can emerge in a professional setting. Professional isolation, instability, or distrust continue to build quickly and are difficult to erase. If you aren't sure what your leader expects of you or what your colleagues think that you are capable of, you are left second-guessing your abilities and talents. While not all lack of communication is career-ending, it is something that can create a slow creep of dissention.

The confusion created when you receive multiple messages about the same topic or erroneous information that you relied on to your own dismay suggests that you may be the problem—that your filter for seeking information has failed time and time again and that you should not be trusted to make any meaningful decisions. This type of self-doubt is clearly driven by external sources but can be so deeply engrained that a talented individual quickly loses confidence.

As professionals, we desire to engage in collaborative conversation. It seems quite simple to suggest that many of the problems raised throughout this chapter with the complexity of communication, the increasing work hours where responsiveness is not only suggested but expected, and where there is opportunity for wrong information to be spread quickly can be solved with regular, meaningful conversations, but they can at least be somewhat reduced in impact. This is not an evaluative setting like a performance review, but rather ongoing collaborative conversations about the daily goings-on of the campus, where questions flow freely and speaking up is encouraged. This type of collaborative conversation can be individual but can also encompass groups and should allow for an organic flow—whether it be from leader to follower, from colleague to colleague, from department to department, or from teacher to student.

Being present and available to others builds confidence in the routes of communication that are established. It corrects outdated paths and directs others to reliable sources of information. It promotes inquiry and curiosity for the sake of growth and engagement rather than discouraging participation through gossip and hearsay.

ACTIVITY: THE 7 Cs OF COMMUNICATION IN HIGHER EDUCATION

The 7 Cs of Communication were introduced in 1952 by Scott Cutlip and Allen Center in their textbook, *Effective Public Relations*. The list was developed to help improve professional communication skills in the advertising industry. The original list has been revised over the years but has remained consistent in the purpose of providing individuals with guidance on how to create clear messages to those whom you interact with either verbally or in a written format.

In Table 2.1 you will find a list of the 7Cs of Communication and a description of each element in the left column (Krishna, 2018). In the right column, you will respond with a plus sign (+) for areas that you feel you are proficient in and a minus sign (–) for areas that need attention to support professional sustainability.

After reviewing the plus (+) and minus (–) signs, use the list included in Table 2.2 to brainstorm strategies that could support you in becoming a stronger communicator related to each of the 7 Cs of Communication. Place a check mark in the box by the strategies that you would like to implement into your future verbal and written communication (Krishna, 2018).

Table 2.1 Ranking 7 Cs of Communication

7 Cs of Communication	Ranking
	(+) for areas that you feel you are proficient in (−) for areas that need attention to support professional sustainability
Clarity—The message should be delivered clearly in simple language.	
Correctness—The message should be delivered with facts and with proper grammar, punctuation, spelling, and semantics.	
Conciseness—The message should be delivered with brevity using short sentences, avoiding wordy expressions and repetition.	
Concreteness—The message should be clear, specific, and provide facts.	
Completeness—The message should provide all the necessary information to answer all possible questions that could be asked.	
Consideration—The message should be created by putting yourself in the receiver's place, using empathy to connect with the receiver.	
Courtesy—The message should be friendly, open, honest, and avoid negativity.	

Source: Author created.

Table 2.2 Strategies for Improving the 7 Cs of Communication

7 Cs of Communication	Strategies to Improve Communication
	Place a check mark in the box by the strategies that you would like to implement into your future verbal and written communication.
Clarity—The message should be delivered clearly in simple language.	❑ Speak slowly. ❑ Do not use jargon or slang. ❑ Use familiar words ❑ When writing, follow the one paragraph–one idea approach. ❑ When writing, minimize the number of ideas in each sentence.
Correctness—The message should be delivered with facts and with proper grammar, punctuation, spelling, and semantics.	❑ Accurate facts should be provided. ❑ Select nondiscriminatory expressions. ❑ Ensure spelling is correct. ❑ Ensure grammar is correct. ❑ Ensure punctuation is correct.
Conciseness—The message should be delivered with brevity using short sentences, avoiding wordy expressions and repetition.	❑ Keep the message brief. ❑ Keep the message truthful. ❑ Avoid wordy expressions. ❑ Avoid repetition in the message. ❑ Eliminate filler words.
Concreteness—The message should be clear, specific, and provide facts.	❑ Be authentic when delivering the message. ❑ Avoid vague expressions. ❑ Use words that can't be misinterpreted. ❑ Provide specific details and facts. ❑ Be specific rather than general.
Completeness—The message should provide all the necessary information to answer all possible questions that could be asked.	❑ Provide answers to all possible questions. ❑ Include facts. ❑ Provide relevant information. ❑ Provide complete information. ❑ Answer the five Ws—who, what, when, where, and why.
Consideration—The message should be created by putting yourself in the receiver's place, using empathy to connect with the receiver.	❑ Put yourself in the receiver's place. ❑ Empathize with the receiver. ❑ Consider the receiver's needs. ❑ Consider the receiver's emotions. ❑ Consider the receiver's viewpoint.

(continued)

Table 2.2 Strategies for Improving the 7 Cs of Communication (*continued*)

7 Cs of Communication	Strategies to Improve Communication
Courtesy—The message should be friendly, open, honest, and avoid negativity.	❑ Create a friendly message. ❑ Create an honest message. ❑ Avoid negativity. ❑ Use politically correct language. ❑ Select words that demonstrate respect.

Source: Author created; adapted from Krishna's journal article "Decoding 7C's in Effective Communication."

CONCLUSION

Communication is an area that encompasses every aspect of our professional and personal lives. We communicate to survive, to collaborate, to better understand, and even to feed intellectual curiosity. Yet the demands that today's higher education professional face can be intensely overwhelming—from never truly being able to "disconnect" to navigating confusing and unclear pathways of messaging. There is no "perfect" communicator; rather, there is a professional routine of prioritizing communication in a way that promotes protecting your own boundaries while also walking alongside those with common goals. By maintaining a clear understanding of how, when, and why communication interferes with professional sustainability, you can better control the boundaries you place around how and when you will communicate.

REFLECTION QUESTIONS

1. As you think about different communication challenges and opportunities you have experienced in higher education, what have you learned?
2. Consider the various ways you receive and share information in your professional life. How can you recognize and clarify communication channels that seem complex or confusing?
3. Think about your communication habits and preferences. How can you better utilize your preferred methods of communication to help others understand you and your intentions?
4. How might you adapt your use of technology to build a better work–life balance?
5. What are some things you can do differently now that you've considered the 7 Cs and your professional sustainability, both as the communicator and on the receiving side of information?

CHAPTER 3

Role Clarity or Lack Thereof

WHY WE STRUGGLE WITH ROLE CLARITY IN HIGHER EDUCATION

Role clarity, or the clear understanding of one's job responsibilities and boundaries, seems to plague faculty in higher education. A new hire enters a position after applying to a job advertisement with a set list of duties and responsibilities, sometimes with the added phrase "other duties as assigned." Yet once onboard, tasks pile on, colleagues shift to other duties, and, proven competent, your own plate becomes overloaded with things you did not expect to take on within your role. Lack of role clarity comes from a variety of places: poor leadership, exceptional talent, reduction in available personnel, and increasing demands from institutions. Wherever your lack of role clarity originates, it most likely forces you to prioritize tasks, reduce emphasis on things you may once have cared deeply about, and learn new skill sets. In all, a lack of role clarity can provide a chance to learn new skills and to grow within a career, but alternatively, it can also stretch an already overworked leader.

A lack of role clarity can be unsettling for most higher education professionals who aspire to do well in their careers. Initially, taking on additional tasks or responsibilities beyond one's typical job scope can be temporary and helpful to the larger cause (the team, the department, the institution). Over time, however, "job creep" can settle in, when what once were temporary responsibilities become a regular occurrence and do not seem to be shifting even after careful consideration from leadership. These new tasks take time away from your other responsibilities, may have priorities and deadlines within themselves, and might even fall out of your skill set.

THE FULL PLATE OF WORKLOAD

Workload is identified as a common cause of workplace stress and burnout—we think of this as a full dinner plate. Anyone working in higher education most likely feels this challenge on today's campuses. We tend to manage our own workloads given the specific responsibilities that we face—and in most cases, our dinner plates can comfortably hold all of these. But there are also times when we are extremely busy with projects and a long to-do list and suddenly get handed an important, immediate need from the college executive team. Then we shift our responsibilities to fit more on our plate. We push side dishes into one another. We start stacking the roast beef on top of the potatoes, and we begin to overlap what we currently can maintain to bring these new items on the plate.

Over time, just like our dinner plates, our workload plate becomes too crowded. A piece of broccoli falls over the edge, the roast beef grows cold, and mixing the corn and mashed potatoes becomes less than appealing. We start missing deadlines or producing average-quality work simply to get a task done. We become forgetful, resentful, and tired. We aren't meant to stack our work dinner plates with heaping mounds of food—there is a balance to how much can reasonably fit, and when we go beyond that, we start losing the boundaries of how well we can do our jobs.

THE CONFUSION OF ROLE CLARITY

Being able to articulate what you do, how your work is measured, and how you fit into the institution seems like a simple task. But, over time, the longer one stays in higher education, whether in a traditional faculty role or in an administrative position, defining the boundaries of your job can become difficult. Add to this the tightening of institutional budgets where employees leaving jobs are not always replaced and job duties are absorbed by others in the areas.

Consider a typical faculty position at a university. Generally, there are set expectations like an established course load, committee responsibilities, research agendas, and service to complete. Over time, as enrollment increases, the faculty member takes on an additional course as overload (and with it comes the need for more projects to grade, office hours to hold, and less time for other tasks). Then, a faculty colleague retires, so you are asked to head the faculty search process—again, on top of everything else you are already doing. This list goes on and on—becoming department chair, taking on administrative duties, and leading assessment processes are just a few possibilities.

The add-on of tasks is one facet of role confusion—who do I serve and what is my priority? But there's an internal war waging as well. How do I succeed at my job without taking on these extra responsibilities? Will I be viewed as someone not willing to go the extra mile for my job? Will I lose future promotion opportunities because I cannot handle one more task today? We often do not notice when job creep starts moving into our mental and physical space, but when we finally do, it is often at the point of overload or exhaustion.

The blame for lack of role clarity does not fall on anyone's shoulders—it happens in every institution to nearly every employee at one point or another. But when we fail to recognize it within our own space, we then start spiraling toward being unable to prioritize, missing deadlines, and performing much below how we want to.

AM I BEING TOO NICE?

Most jobs have some blurry areas of expectations that go beyond a specific list of responsibilities. In our own roles as faculty, we've led admissions committees, designed new courses, and participated in campus fundraisers—all of which were not required but were helpful to engaging with the campus community. There's something inherently natural about investing in your institution, and it seems that many who end up working and leading in higher education tend to be the type of people who are willing to do what it takes to get the job done, even if it means stretching their own expertise or taking on extra work. Humility, it seems, is likely rewarded over time.

This good-natured spirit of willingness to take on extra duties while someone is out of the office or to split responsibilities after a colleague's retirement can be productive and cost-saving. Certainly, if institutions can save money by reducing the number of people on the payroll, it is advantageous. Yet recent studies, particularly after the COVID-19 pandemic in 2020, specify lack of role clarity as one of the primary causes of job stress and burnout (Koster & McHenry, 2023). One professor considering leaving academia noted that after the pandemic, "there were often messages coming into some of the spaces that I was in that 'you have to do more with less'" (Flaherty, 2022).

DON'T LET THE AMBIANCE FOOL YOU

Very few jobs allow complete autonomy for the employee; however, working in higher education is known to have advantages that are not typical in most corporate or nonacademic settings. Being able to pursue your own research interests, conducting classes using the ways you teach best, and the somewhat easy-natured coming and going of campus offices can make academia seem like a peaceful, easygoing environment. Yet peek behind those office doors or into those administrative meetings and you are likely to find exhausted and overworked individuals.

ACTIVITY: CONSIDERING AND PROTECTING YOUR TALENTS

It is important to recognize that roles evolve over time as the landscape of higher education changes. To help provide clarity around your position, we developed the Higher Education Role Map (HERM), a visual brainstorming activity that can assist in gaining clarity around your role by enabling you to identify your ongoing responsibilities, better understand the role of your team and how you interact with key collaborators, your special projects, and key outcome metrics. HERM is inspired by well-known visual techniques such as mind mapping and concept mapping. Mind maps provide a structured way to organize ideas and information. The general goal of mind maps is to help understand complicated concepts by breaking them down into their most basic elements. The mind mapping technique can be used to develop new ideas or to break down and better understand existing information, whereas concept maps, according to Davies (2011), are more structured and less pictorial in nature. The aim of concept maps is not to generate spontaneous associations but to outline relationships between already established ideas. The HERM process intermixes the mind mapping element of breaking down the complexities of your role with the concept map's focus of identifying the relationships between all the intricacies of your position.

According to Hilary Jane Grosskopf (2018), author of *Awake Leadership*, a role mapping diagram should start with you as the main focus of the role map. While Grosskopf's work was more specific to the retail industry, HERM has been adapted to relate to higher education. The objective of the HERM process is to identify your role's entire scope to use as a tool for self-awareness and self-reflection and to share with leadership to guide the conversation about role clarity. The categories include:

- **Tasks:** These include your ongoing responsibilities, everything you do on a consistent basis each day, week, month, semester, or academic year.
- **Team Members:** These are individuals with whom you directly collaborate on a frequent basis to support your position.
- **Collaborators:** These individuals, offices, or programs can be either internal or external to your institution and provide support or a service for your program, department, or office.
- **Special Projects:** The projects you are currently working on as one-time efforts.
- **Metrics:** Outcome measures that you use to track individual, program, department, or office progress.

To create your HERM, follow these instructions:

Step 1: Draw a circle in the center of your page. In the center of this circle, write your name and title. Then create five smaller circles that are connected with lines to the original circle you drew with your name and title. Label the circles Tasks, Team Members, Collaborators, Special Projects, and Metrics.

Step 2: In the "Tasks" circle list your ongoing responsibilities. It may be easier to divide the circle into several sections and identify your responsibilities by daily, weekly, semester, or academic year intervals. It is important to create this circle in a way that is authentic to your role.

Step 3: In the "Team Members" circle, write the names and titles of the individuals with whom you work closely on a frequent basis to carry out your key responsibilities. These individuals could be direct reports, colleagues with similar roles, faculty, or staff. List their main roles and responsibilities as you know them that help support your role.

Step 4: In the "Key Collaborators" circle, think about the internal people or groups you collaborate with to support your role, program, or department but don't work directly with you every day such as cross-departmental teams, marketing, enrollment, career services, student services, or admissions. Also, what external stakeholders do you collaborate with? This might include community-based organizations, consulting organizations, or advisory boards. Write their names and titles in this circle, along with details about how you work in partnership with each key collaborator.

Step 5: In the "Special Projects" circle, write down any projects you're currently working on that are one-time efforts or are outside of your routine tasks and responsibilities. Examples might be launching a new program, writing a grant proposal, developing a new course, or writing an article for submission. Include an estimated completion date for each special project.

Step 6: In the "Metrics" circle, list the data points you use to measure success in your role. List outcome measures or key performance indicators you use to track the progress of your role, program, department, or office. This could include data points such as student enrollment, progression, retention rates, feedback surveys, financial reports, or student surveys.

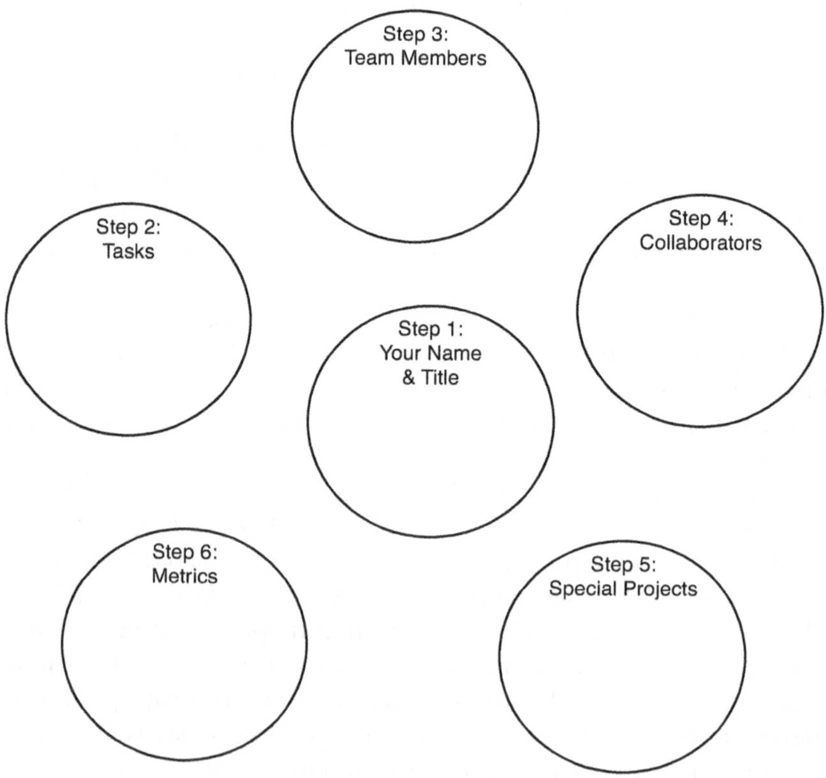

Once you have completed your HERM visual, reflect on the following questions:

- What surprised you most about your diagram?
- How does your map align with the overall goals of your program, department, and institution?
- Are there any areas where you feel uncertain about your role or responsibilities?
- Are there components of your position that could be delegated to someone else?
- If you could change one thing on your HERM, what would it be? Why?

Now that you have a better understanding regarding the scope of your position, consider this checklist to review areas that might be lacking in role clarity in your professional life.

- ❑ **Review your HERM with your leader or trusted colleague:** Have a conversation with your leader about changes in your role and responsibilities.
- ❑ **Participate in regular check-ins with colleagues:** Discuss job responsibilities, clarify any doubts, and receive honest feedback on role performance (Garr, 2022).
- ❑ **Offer team role clarification sessions:** Offer regular opportunities for discussions within teams to share about their roles and how they collaborate with others, both internally and external to the institution.
- ❑ **Clarify decision-making power:** Ensure employees understand their decision-making authority and the boundaries of their role.
- ❑ **Identify role overload:** Assess whether employees are experiencing job creep (too many responsibilities).
- ❑ **Establish feedback loops:** Create continuous feedback loops to monitor whether role clarity is being maintained.

By using either a single strategy or a combination of the strategies provided, you can assess and enhance role clarity, both for yourself and those you lead, resulting in improved performance, reduced confusion, and increased job satisfaction among employees.

CONCLUSION

Roles in higher education are constantly changing. Even if you remain in the same position year after year, there is a high probability that you have experienced job creep when a colleague left a position and you inherited some of their responsibilities or as the nature of education changed your skill set grew. The ability to multitask, to work across departments or divisions, or to be trusted with new responsibilities can be a very positive thing. The challenge is in recognizing when it is interfering with your ability to do quality work as opposed to a lot of work. Always protect your time so that you can be the best at what you do and in that become an advocate not only to raise an awareness of job creep but to advocate for an awareness that role confusion can be a detriment to overall institutional progress.

REFLECTION QUESTIONS

1. How has your current role evolved over time? Was the change slow or did it happen quickly? How did the change affect your self-care practices?
2. How would you describe role clarity to a colleague?
3. What will you do to enhance the clarity of your role?
4. How will you enhance role clarity for those who you lead?
5. What are some things you can do differently now that you've considered role clarity and your professional sustainability?

CHAPTER 4

Lack of Control

WHY DO WE STRUGGLE WITH LACK OF CONTROL IN OUR HIGHER EDUCATION CAREERS?

It might seem surprising, but a long-term professional life in higher education can defy the public perception of a somewhat easy and predictable professional journey. When we, the authors, were in our undergraduate years, we recall our professors and campus leaders holding lifetime positions with what appeared to be minimal stress and a lifetime guarantee of work. Hollywood productions helped this assumption with stories of lives on college campuses where faculty were seen meeting with students under the large oak tree in the center of campus or wielding a sharp tongue during a classroom lecture. What could be easier than sitting in a comfy, campus office chatting with students about intellectual topics, writing a research article every now and then, and socializing at campus gatherings? At times, there might be rumblings of a disgruntled professor challenging the status quo or disagreements between students and instructors, but all in all, the life of a professor has long been viewed publicly as a comfortable and stable life ambition.

Many struggle with lack of control in higher education. A Gallup survey found that 45% of today's professionals have no clarity on what is expected of them at work (Wigert & Tatel, 2024). As a result, employees feel confused as there are no clear definitions of what is considered success in the workplace. The causes for this lack of clarity come from five recent evolutions in the workplace, and we've applied these to changes in higher education to better understand the relevance of these issues:

(a) Rapid organizational change. Colleges and universities have faced budget cuts, political demands, changes in student populations, increasing regulation from external entities, and an increasing demand to compete for students. Even faculty in tenured positions have no clear job security. Campuses are adding remote learning options, adult education pathways, and new majors to meet the demands of today's workforce. This changes the daily function of a leader in that nothing is predictably consistent and even those things that could be could face a sudden upheaval based on the changing winds in higher education. Organizational change causes individuals to frequently question job stability, commitment to the organization, and even willingness to step up to lead when change is on the horizon.

(b) The switch to a hybrid or remote work environment. Over the last two decades, the wide use of distance learning and online learning systems has created new programming, opportunities to recruit and retain students, and venues for faculty employment. This switch, however, did not happen quickly and without minimal care. Leaders in higher education were forced to build policy structures that supported both face-to-face and online learning, to provide professional development for faculty and staff working in these environments, and to understand ways to assess performance in a hybrid or remote environment.

(c) A change in the expectations of others outside the organization. Institutions of higher education, while educationally based in mission and strategy, do serve the needs and demands of outside academic partners. Students demand more for their increasing tuition dollars, parents sending their young adults to school seek employability after investing in education, and employers seek a productive and agile workforce of graduates. Kevin McClure, faculty at the University of North Carolina-Wilmington stated,

> We're in the middle of an incredibly dynamic labor market. There are lots of companies and organizations that are looking for talent, and there are people in higher education who have had an incredibly difficult experience over the last couple of years that are looking at those opportunities in a different way. Even though these problems have existed for a long time, not paying attention to them now could have even more dire consequences for institutions than it did previously (Lederman, 2022, para. 14).

These expectations trickle back to leaders in that there is a constant demand for change—to prove educational worth, to change class structures to meet changing learning needs, and to better understand the job market.

(d) A demand on employees to navigate change quickly and with little direction. Particularly in higher education, change often requires innovation and creativity. What is being asked of leaders is to think in new and creative ways—to save money while doing more, to recruit more students with less tuition discounts, and to fill courses and yet achieve similar learning outcomes. Colleges and universities often do not have internal resources to guide change; rather, change occurs when policies or practices are mandated or suggested, and the implementation part is passed down to the individual leaders and departments to struggle with how to get it done. The need for quick responses that are also mistake-free can lead to a high-pressure work environment with little acknowledgment for jobs well done.

(e) Incoherent ways of measuring success (Wigert & Tatel, 2024). A Gallup poll suggests that most employees have little faith in their employer's performance measurement system—and this is common in higher education. Tenured faculty tend to undergo less frequent reviews than untenured faculty, adjunct faculty may participate in limited employee supervision, and other campus personnel may only face annual performance reviews that affirm the status quo rather than home in on professional development goals.

The reality of a lack of control within higher education settings does not necessarily indicate that campuses lack leadership or structure, but rather that conditions and times change rapidly and that the employees working on those campuses must adapt quickly. Without considering the impact of frequent or sudden change on employee satisfaction or performance, leaders miss the opportunities to better guide a sustainable integration of new processes into campus culture.

LACK OF CONTROL ON THE INDIVIDUAL LEVEL

If change is inevitable and professionals in higher education are expected to be fluid and flexible in their resistance to change, it is wise to consider what this means to the individual who, on a day-to-day basis, faces a lack of control within his or her individual role. While the larger impact on campuses has been caused by shifts in demands for different types of learning and responses to political and budgetary demands, the individual employee has little to no opportunity to provide feedback or resistance to these changes. Thus, if you want to continue to work in higher education, the expectation is that you will adapt and adjust.

On the individual job level, lack of control can show up in a variety of ways from feeling helpless and hopeless to low productivity. One common trait is that employees feel like they have little to no say in what happens in the workplace; that is, decisions are being made "around" them, and their input is not sought or solicited and, as such, not valued. Examples of this might be increasing or changing course loads, having no input on flexibility in work hours or remote work options, experiencing heightened scrutiny on classroom practices, or being subjected to budget decisions that disrupt day-to-day practices. Joshua Kim, reporter for the website Inside Higher Ed identified some of these practices in 2017 as "The Casual Disparagement of Higher Ed Staff." In that article, Kim noted that the depth of loyalty of many who work in higher education is not rewarded. He wrote, "higher ed staff come to work each day committed to do whatever it takes to advance the goals—and the financial resilience—of the institutions [where] we work. Staff are true believers in the missions of our institutions, and of the promise of higher education as a creator of opportunity" (para. 8). Yet no amount of belief in the mission or commitment to the bigger goals of an institution provides clarity on one's day-to-day responsibilities, leading, in turn, to job dissatisfaction and feelings of unappreciation and unworthiness.

One campus trend we've noticed regarding lack of control occurs when employees leave and are not replaced—this might be staff turnover, faculty lines being vacated but not filled, or administrative offices remaining empty for months or years at a time. These types of vacancies can provide immediate budget savings and a perception of downsizing to a more efficient and economical model. However, when this happens, responsibilites typically fall on the shoulders of coworkers or associates. As employees leave, the roles of those left behind are multiplied—sometimes quite substantially. If you are one of these employees, you feel the pressure of an increasing workload with little hope of ever going back to the norm and instead being forced to adapt to doing more with fewer resources.

Another noticeable campus trend is the lack of alignment between evaluation practices and actual duties. A typical faculty member may face a contracted workload of 60% teaching, 20% research, and 20% service (depending on the role, these percentages vary across institutions, but the premise remains the same). While these numbers seem straightforward, many things arise during an academic year that do not clearly fit in any category or that go unaccounted for in the overall workload. Consider daily tasks like emailing students, attending committee meetings, rewriting a journal article submission, or hosting a lunch for alumni. These day-to-day tasks are at the heart of the institution's work yet are often not significant enough to be listed on a curriculum vitae or accounted for in a performance evaluation heavily reliant on student reviews and publication numbers. In that, the tasks being used for performance evaluation often undermine the more tedious work that keeps the institutional machine afloat. Lack of alignment between evaluation practices and reality also causes uncomfortable performance review sessions between leaders and their colleagues. A once-a-year evaluation meeting leaves little room for actual professional development and growth. Additionally, in some situations where evaluation is conducted based on a prepopulated form or rubric, evaluation is based more on a look at past practices rather than on anticipated growth or personal goals. As an employee undergoing an annual review, the interaction can feel cold and unmotivating—thus reinforcing the lack of control that is already felt in uncertain circumstances.

HOW LACK OF CONTROL IMPACTS OUR CAREER SUSTAINABILITY AND SELF-CARE

Demoralization is often the result when one feels a lack of control in the workplace. Demoralization refers "to a state where employees feel disheartened, lacking motivation and confidence in their work" (Sarasa, 2025, para. 1). The Mayo Clinic (2025) suggests that an employee feels something akin to burnout, or feeling "useless, powerless and empty" (para. 1). When a person feels like they do not matter in the decision-making process, they lose the ambition to build a long career in that same place where their opinion is not valued or sought.

Lack of control on a personal level often leads to poor work–life balance, increasing workloads with less output, increased absenteeism, and lack of passion for one's work. Having little no input into decision-making causes disconnection and exhaustion. In all, lack of control has no notable outcomes for anyone in higher education. It muddies relationships, slows movement toward strategic goals, and causes conflict within workspaces. It's worth noting that 60% of those looking to leave their current position say they wouldn't seek opportunities at their current institution (Fuesting & Schneider, 2023).

Another way lack of control manifests around our self-care and career sustainability in higher education is unpredictably of promotion and advancement opportunities. *The Chronicle of Higher Education* discussed this as "feeling trapped in a dead-end job" (Chronicle of Higher Education, 2022, para. 2). With budget cuts causing reduction in staff and older workers staying further into retirement-eligible years, opportunities for job promotion can be rare. That same 2022 survey reported in *The Chronicle of Higher Education* stated, "Academic department heads and deans are often identified through national searches, while administrative deans/directors and department heads are often pursued with a 'who can we get for the least money that will do the most work' mind-set" (para. 15). In that, employees who will overwork for less cost are valued over employees who demand fair compensation for the work they complete.

More personally, lack of control can heighten physical and mental wellness issues for someone stuck in a role where they feel they have little to no control. The Mayo Clinic (2023) suggests lack of control may lead to feelings of isolation, dissatisfaction, inability to sleep well, and/or increased alcohol use. The American Institute of Stress reports that "workers who perceive they are subjected to high demands but have little control are at increased risk for cardiovascular disease" (American Institute of Stress, 2025, para. 1). Working in conditions where you feel a lack of control can be quite detrimental on a personal level.

Leaders in higher education can engage in several strategies to help alleviate the feelings of lack of control of not only their own workload but that of their colleagues. First, leaders should acknowledge what is in their control and what is not—both personally and professionally. Acknowledging that decisions are being made of and about your job without your input allows for a recognition that even at an ideal situation or a role, there will always be things that you cannot control. Second, leaders can recognize when an employee or colleague is impacted by decisions that cause their workload to increase, their role to shift, or their responsibilities to divide. Openly acknowledging and inviting conversation about these changes can reduce the feelings of helplessness and serve as an acknowledgement that lack of control is not only recognized by the one affected but by others as well. In a way, the leader can help moderate the discussion about why decisions are made and how the impact of those decisions can best be managed with minimal impact.

Additionally, leaders can advocate and move more strategically in decision-making. Instead of instituting widespread change, include multiple stakeholders in the conversation who specifically pay attention to how various roles change and how those roles can take part in the change process. Leaders can invite feedback about role clarity—where it is present and where it is not. In this, employees can explain things that the leader may not notice in everyday interactions or advocate for a better balance of work-based responsibilities.

ACTIVITY: CIRCLE OF CONTROL

The Circle of Control is a framework that helps to differentiate between things you can directly control, those you can only influence, or those you can't control at all (Schaffner, 2023). As leaders in higher education, the Circle of Control can be helpful to navigate your roles and responsibilities while maintaining a sense of empowerment, balance, and seeking professional sustainability.

Things I Can Control. The first and smallest circle in the center represents aspects of our life that we have direct control over. These include our thoughts, beliefs, emotions, interpretations, and perceptions of our lived experiences (Schaffner, 2023). Additionally, in higher education are the following list of items that are generally in your control:

- **Leadership:** You control how you approach leadership roles.
- **Time management:** You decide how you manage your time.
- **Setting boundaries:** You control how you set boundaries to maintain work–life balance.
- **Career growth:** You are responsible for shaping your career trajectory by seeking opportunities relevant to your professional aspirations.
- **Networking:** You have control over who you build relationships with within your program, department, institution, and industry.

- **Teaching elements:** You determine which textbooks, journal articles, and online resources are most appropriate for your courses.
- **Assessment methods:** You decide how students are evaluated, for example, exams, papers, projects, discussion boards, or participation.
- **Research and scholarship:** You can determine the directions of your research and how you share your findings.

Things I Can Influence. The second circle, or the circle of influence, represents the intersection between things within our immediate control and those that fall outside of our area of control (Schaffner, 2023). It is important to recognize that we can control our efforts in this circle, but not necessarily the outcomes or the final result. A few examples might include:

- **Course design:** You have control over how you design and deliver courses. You don't have control over how your students use the information to complete course assignments or study for exams.
- **Professional development:** You have control over your efforts to stay updated in your field, attend conferences, participate in workshops, and pursue continuing education. You do not have control over how fast the content changes in your field.
- **Work–life balance:** You have control over how you manage your time, set boundaries between work and personal life, and take care of your well-being. You do not have control over how others feel about your approach to work–life balance.

Things Outside My Control. The third and largest circle are things we deeply care about but are out of our control (Schaffner, 2023). Examples related to higher education could include:

- **Institutional decisions:** Changes in funding, tuition rates, or leadership policies are out of your control, but they might impact your work environment, teaching, or research.
- **Political issues:** Changes in views regarding higher education.
- **Global issues:** This might include things like a health crisis, similar to COVID-19.

HOW TO USE THE CIRCLE OF CONTROL

Step 1: Using the image provided in Figure 4.1, draw three circles and label them Things I Can Control, Things I Can Influence, and Things Outside My Control.

Step 2: Start reflecting on the innermost circle, **Things I Can Control.** Acknowledge that you have the power to shape certain aspects of your life. Start listing all the things that you have control over—these are things that you can do something about right now. If you are having a hard time getting started, think through the various roles you manage on a day-to-day basis, such as administrating, teaching, research, and so on.

Step 3: Begin brainstorming for the next circle, **Things I Can Influence.** While you can't directly control everything, identify where you can make a difference. List the things you can influence.

Step 4: Complete the outermost circle, **Things Outside My Control.** List the things or issues you care deeply about but can't change. It's important to recognize these things or issues without letting them overwhelm you.

Figure 4.1 Circle of Control

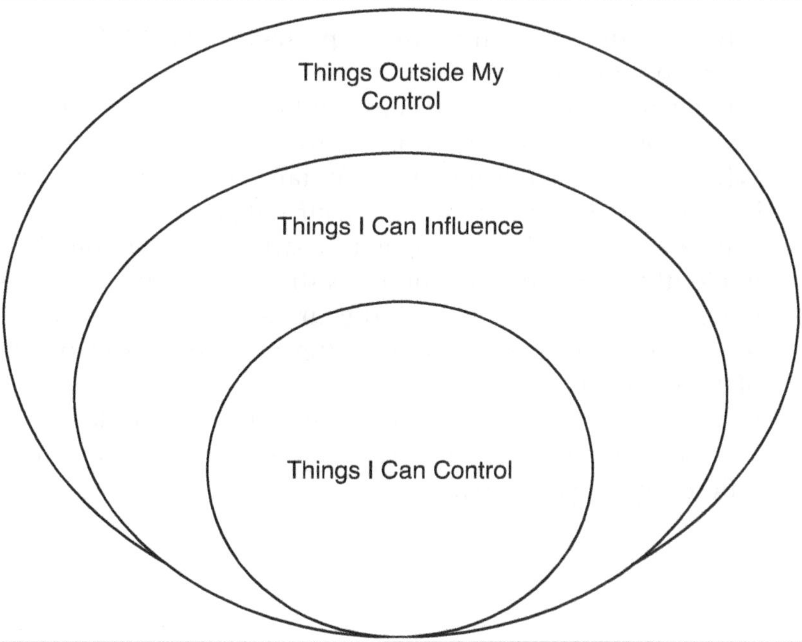

Source: Created by Vicki Bautista.

By regularly using the Circle of Control to assess things you can directly control, those you can only influence, or those you can't control at all, you can find greater clarity on how to navigate professional life in higher education.

CONCLUSION

It may be good to recognize that even professionals occupying the highest leadership roles lack control of many things in their professional and personal lives. Control, and lack thereof, is a universal human experience, and we can better manage our response to it when we are aware there is tension. Control should never be used as a means of manipulation, nor should it be used as a method to cause harm to someone; instead, it should be embraced as a way of recognizing that we cannot demand perfection in any given situation. Our best approach is to recognize this and to prepare ourselves to be open to the opportunity to learn from situations.

REFLECTION QUESTIONS

1. What is within my control in my professional life? What is clearly out of my control?
2. What professional growth steps can I take to better manage my response to things I cannot control?
3. Who is a trusted colleague you can talk to when control or lack of control begins to impact your self-care?
4. Why is control a challenging issue, particularly for you? Begin to identify situations or conditions that raise your awareness where control might be up in the air and start to formulate a few steps you can engage in to better understand the dynamics of control in the situation.
5. Now that you've learned a bit about control and lack of control in higher education, what are some things you can do differently moving forward?

CHAPTER 5

The Desire for Meaningful Recognition

WHY DO WE STRUGGLE WITH MEANINGFUL RECOGNITION IN HIGHER EDUCATION CAREERS?

Feeling valued because of our work is one reason many of us stay in the professions we do. While it is reported that many leave jobs in higher education in search of higher pay, many stay for their entire careers. Money, it seems, can drive some decision-making, but not for all. Some stay working in colleges and universities because they see a potential for career growth, they have a passion for working with students, or they find a niche for their skill set to be utilized to help the larger organization. A study from Gallup (2024) found that employee recognition motivates, provides a sense of accomplishment, and makes employees feel valued for their work. The research also found that recognition not only boosts individual employee engagement but has been found to increase productivity and loyalty to the company, leading to professional sustainability.

USA Today published an article in 2013 titled "5 Reasons to Consider a Career in Higher Education." In this article, contributor Gretchen Edwards considered the career possibilities that exist within colleges and universities and listed five reasons that might draw new employees into institutions: (1) the variety of roles beyond teaching, including marketing, art, recruitment, budgeting, or facilities management; (2) developing a diverse skill set as many jobs at higher education institutions require working across departments or collaborating with different groups; (3) the availability of cultural and educational offerings; (4) learning the ropes of how institutions are run like businesses—so the principles of accounting, balancing a budget, and financing are common topics of high interest across campus; and (5) being part of something larger—that is, contributing to the process of education and being part of a structure that helps others accomplish their goals. In the 12 years since that publication, these same possibilities remain true—even in the face of expanding education options, varied work styles, and increasing demands for accountability.

Interestingly enough, very few are asked what meaningful recognition would look like to them in their professional workspace. Only 10% of employees report being asked about their preferences for receiving recognition, and as noted by organizations Gallup and Workhuman, "the education industry is no exception to the lack of individualization and authenticity that can happen when recognition isn't done right" (Kuncl & Christiansen, 2024, para. 17).

We do admit that money is nice. Very nice. Professionals in higher education deserve to be paid at fair rates and to be recognized monetarily for the work that they do. But we also know that many institutions are unable to keep up with market rates of pay, and thus spending a career in higher education sometimes means also earning less than you could in other organizations. Regardless, institutions have turned to ways to try to reward or recognize awards in nonmonetary ways—free swag, pizza parties, flexible work schedules, and other mechanisms that do not hold a hefty price tag, and while these are efforts, they often fall short of what professionals truly desire: meaningful recognition.

ASSUMPTIONS ABOUT RECOGNITION

What we are expected to do in higher education roles—whether they be faculty, staff, or administrative—is to seek meaning in our work regardless of recognition. Part of this can be tied to the type of work that we do—serving others. Thirty-five percent of university professionals often feel burned out (Kuncl & Christiansen, 2024). One reason for this is that working in education requires a good amount of selflessness and attention to others. While we agree that our primary role is one invested in caring for others and promoting a safe, caring learning environment, we also should not do so at the detriment to ourselves. The assumptions around higher education professionals are that we should be so deeply invested in our research, our commitment to the institution, or our desire to reach students that we overflow with gratitude just to be on campus. Any outward vocalization or demand for recognition is seen as self-promoting or greedy.

The CUPA-HR 2023 Higher Education Employee Retention Survey found that the most important facets of job satisfaction are recognition and feeling valued (Bichsel et al., 2023). These two facets were indicators of the likelihood if an individual would stay or leave a job at an institution of higher education. Notably, the same survey found that individuals seeking to find employment were not looking to leave higher education, but rather to find a different position within their own institution or within another institution of higher education. In sum, there does not seem to be a mass exodus of professionals who want to leave higher education, but rather professionals who want to know that their work matters and is valued.

Let us not forget that earlier statistic—only 10% of employees are ever outright asked what their ideal form of recognition would be—which leaves room for a lot of guessing and trial by error by leaders. A shout-out via email for a job well done may leave one professional satisfied with the reach of recognition, while another may be underwhelmed by the lack of specificity or individuality.

However, the drive for recognition is also paired with the need for career stability and survival. For faculty, recognition of a well-written article or a positive teaching review supports measures that lead to promotion and tenure. Faculty, in many senses, are taught to compete—for funding resources, for grants, for higher position, or for awards that recognize their efforts above others. Some are trained in the "publish or perish" mentality where the only way to keep a faculty role is through an ambitious research agenda. Unfair treatment like favoritism or lack of professional guidance perpetuates the expectation that recognition is only earned. This mindset gives implicit permission to rise above others for the sake of career survival.

In nonfaculty roles, the drive for recognition is primarily focused on career advancement, pay increases, and personal satisfaction. Being recognized as someone who stands out at your job sends a message to others that you are an asset to the institution and also helps support an internal dialogue of worthiness and capability. In these roles, however, feedback is based less on public recognition and more so on the day-to-day pats on the back or messages of affirmation or monetary increases in salary. We believe, then, that feedback is accompanied by a reward.

WHAT IS MEANINGFUL RECOGNITION IN HIGHER EDUCATION?

While an affinity for the institution, its people, or virtues may be an impetus to spend an extensive career at a college or university, it is meaningful recognition that can ensure the good people stay. Meaningful recognition is more than a salary increase or a public award (though both of these are important ways to demonstrate value); it is knowing that many stay in higher education because they believe in the mission of educating others and want to be part of that larger process, and feedback takes different forms than in other entities.

Institutions often attempt to provide the three most popular employment benefits like retirement, health insurance, and paid time off. However, CUPA-HR found that nearly 75% of higher education professionals were dissatisfied with employment benefits that were most closely aligned with work–life balance including remote work policies, childcare benefits, and parental leave options.

The American Association of Critical Nursing developed standards for creating positive academic work environments. One aspect of their standards was the notion of creating space for meaningful recognition, which they defined as more than just positive feedback, but recognition that "acknowledges positive behaviors but also includes information about how the impact behaviors have on others, ensuring feedback is relevant to the situation and equal to the person's contribution" (Altman, 2021, para. 4). In their qualitative study of faculty perceptions of recognition, two key aspects about meaningful recognition emerged: it must be genuine, and it must be consistent.

Genuine recognition is timely, specific, and individual. This type of feedback does not have to be publicly shared—it might be words shared between colleagues or a supervisor and employee, but what is important is that it is responsive to an individual's positive contribution. It recognizes the unique personality and traits of the person (if you know someone hates being praised publicly, then do it privately or through a handwritten note). It calls out the specific contribution of the individual and notes exactly what was worthy of recognition—not a general affirmation, but a specific reason the individual's work should be recognized.

Consistent feedback is equally as important as genuine feedback. Ensure that feedback is not directed only at one work group or individual, is spread across campus departments, and is not limited to a certain type of employee (full time vs. part time, faculty vs. adjunct faculty, etc.). One aspect of consistency is that it is seen as representative of the compliment and equates to the recognition or reward. Kuncl and Christiansen (2024) suggest that leaders in education check in at least weekly with their colleagues and, more importantly, listen to their concerns as an opportunity to provide recognition of meaningful feedback.

Furthermore, Gallup (2024) found that beyond communicating appreciation and providing motivation to the recognized employee, the act of recognition also affirms to all professionals what success looks like. In this way, recognition is both a tool for personal reward and an opportunity to reinforce the desired culture of the organization.

FINDING PURPOSE IN PERFORMANCE EVALUATIONS

One misstep we have seen and experienced during our careers in higher education has been the use of routine performance evaluations that have no actual impact on a professional's development. Performance evaluations in the form of quarterly or annual reviews that provide direct assessment of an individual's alignment with predetermined metrics or goals can be helpful, but they should also matter. Some performance evaluation and review processes are exercises in futility—where an evaluator does not want to upset the status quo in a department, so they use performance evaluations to share neutral or positive feedback, while avoiding any harsh or negative comments. Others use performance evaluations as a way to secure an employee's buy-in or job satisfaction, creating a situation where a mediocre employee is praised. Others use performance evaluations to tiptoe around troublesome issues to signal problematic areas but also to ensure an employee doesn't consider leaving a well-oiled machine.

Performance evaluations are not secret. In practice, they may be protected by institutional policies or practices, but nearly always, good employees notice when bad employees are rewarded for their work. They recognize when a leader has avoided a difficult conversation in order to keep the peace, and they also can begin to form a belief structure that neither good nor bad evaluations mean anything. Strong employees grow disgruntled or discouraged and may start acting out because they feel their work is undervalued. Underperforming employees may continue to do so—to the dismay of their colleagues, feeling that their underperformance has gone unnoticed or just does not matter. In any situation, whether overtly shared or not, lack of meaningful and honest performance evaluations is clearly noticed.

To be meaningful, performance evaluations should be personal and collaborative. That is, when a campus professional takes part in a performance evaluation, they should recognize that the feedback was built on their actual performance and contributions. Additionally, the professional should be able to add to their performance review or to challenge assumptions or misconceptions about their work. Gallup's workplace analysis shows that when leaders listen to employee concerns and provide meaningful feedback, they build trust and reduce feelings of inequity. More importantly, performance evaluations should promote professional growth. The professional facing evaluation should be charged with leading the conversation on her own professional growth goals, how those might be measured, and where or how the evaluator can help facilitate those goals. Performance evaluations should provide opportunities for individualization, for the professional to identify areas of needed growth, and for the evaluator and professional to generate best avenues to achieve professional growth goals.

HOW LACK OF MEANINGFUL FEEDBACK IMPACTS OUR SELF-CARE AND PROFESSIONAL SUSTAINABILITY

As professionals, we need (and desire) feedback to better understand what we are doing well and where we have room to grow (and, quite possibly, things that we do not do well at all). Yet when feedback is infrequent or not personal, we lose motivation and can begin to feel like we do not matter to our organization. This, in turn, feeds into lack of drive and decreased productivity.

More concerning in higher education is the lack of meaningful feedback through required performance evaluation processes. We have heard time and again from higher education professionals who attest to annual or biannual reviews being used as one of two things: a way to get rid of a terrible employee or a way to provide generic job performance advice. Neither of these approaches recognizes individual achievements, leadership attributes, or personalized growth opportunities. When an institution fails to use performance processes as a means to provide support and growth for employees, it fails to recognize the importance of this type of feedback in one's professional journey. Beyond formal performance processes, informal feedback is the way we learn about our professional aptitude from day to day. Positive accolades, quick emails of congratulations, smiles across a meeting room table, or even group celebrations provide encouragement and help professionals to immediately connect their actions to the feedback. Negative feedback works the same way—when you know in the moment (or close to it) that your performance is less than ideal, you have a chance to modify your work.

Deborah Grayson Riegel (2019) explored three assumptions professionals might make when they do not receive meaningful feedback. These include assuming that (1) underperforming is acceptable, (2) the leader is afraid to share an honest opinion, or (3) no one cares if professional growth is taking place. Any of these assumptions deters professional growth and, in fact, builds a case for complacency.

More personally, when feedback is not meaningful, it can create conditions for self-doubt, negative self-talk, inaccurate assessments of interpersonal situations, paranoia, and negative feelings about one's worth in the professional setting. These really are the heart of why meaningful feedback is important—it helps us feel valued and like our contributions matter.

ACTIVITY: IDENTIFYING YOUR RECOGNITION STYLE

Consider your own experiences with receiving recognition. Table 5.1 provides space to reflect on and identify your personal preferences for how you like to be recognized for your work, achievements, and contributions with your peers or at the team, department, or institutional level. Understanding your recognition preferences will allow you to better advocate for yourself in the future. Additionally, understanding your own recognition preference will allow you to more easily have the conversation with those whom you lead.

Table 5.1 Exploration of Meaningful Recognition Preferences

Questions	Answers	Notes
	(select as many as applicable)	Use this column to explore your answers in further depth. What influenced your responses? Why does your answer incentivize you?
What do you like to be recognized for?	❑ Role performance ❑ Value to organization ❑ Value to career field specific to role in higher education (work that impacts both higher education and specialized training) ❑ Teamwork or collaboration ❑ Innovation ❑ Ongoing education (certifications, degrees, etc.) ❑ Customer service ❑ Personal accomplishments outside of the workplace	
What type of recognition do you prefer?	❑ Verbal, in person, or via the phone or videoconferencing application ❑ Written, in the form of an email, letter, or card ❑ Recognition from manager/ leader at the relevant level (e.g., department, division, institution) ❑ Private recognition (supervisor and/or other leadership roles provide kudos in private setting) ❑ Public recognition (you are recognized in front of your peers, team, department, or at an institutional level) ❑ On website or social media platform appropriate for workplace recognition at the relevant level (e.g., department, division, institution)	

(*continued*)

Table 5.1 Exploration of Meaningful Recognition Preferences (*continued*)

Questions	Answers	Notes
When would you like to be recognized?	❑ At the completion of a project ❑ Praise along the way ❑ Both	
Do you prefer individual or team recognition?	❑ Individual recognition ❑ Team recognition ❑ Both	
What purpose does recognition serve for you?	❑ Establishes culture norms for expectations ❑ Increases productivity ❑ Enhances position satisfaction ❑ Improves team culture for myself, peers, team, department, or institution ❑ Enhances loyalty to team, department, or institution ❑ Provides sense of security in position/role ❑ Provides motivation to go above and beyond in the future	

Source: Author created.

CONCLUSION

It is not wrong or selfish to seek personalized feedback in your professional role. In fact, it is fair that you should expect this. Yet feedback remains one of those areas that has yet to be perfected, so often institutions either create their own rules or provide feedback in inconsistent and irregular ways. One piece we hope you recognize after reading this chapter is that not all feedback is equal. Some organizations try to reward their employees with pizza parties or t-shirts as a means of recognizing good performance, yet these measures are often perceived as highly impersonal and lacking in specificity for the growing professional. Meaningful, personal feedback is not only a way to better understand your performance but also a way to protect and understand your professional self-worth.

REFLECTION QUESTIONS

1. After completing "Identifying Your Recognition Style," what are your main takeaways about how you like to be recognized at work?
2. Describe a time when someone recognized you and it was meaningful.
3. Describe a time when someone recognized you and it wasn't meaningful. How did that feel different from the time it was meaningful?
4. Describe a time when you weren't recognized and you should have been based on previous organizational precedent. How did that make you feel?
5. Think about a situation in the future where you could potentially be recognized with your peers or at the team, department, or institutional level. How would you like to be recognized in this scenario? Explain why this type of recognition resonates with you.

CHAPTER 6

Lack of Confidence in Leadership

WHY DO WE LACK CONFIDENCE IN OUR LEADERS IN HIGHER EDUCATION CAREERS?

Leading in higher education is not easy, and if we embrace the wider definition that being a leader is inclusive to more than those roles with formal leadership titles, then all of us have a responsibility to lead within the context in which we work. However, organizational hierarchies exist, and individuals do hold leadership positions that can influence job satisfaction, campus conditions, and the future of the institution. In a perfect world, the workforce on a campus would wholeheartedly support leadership (or leadership regime) to lead the institution. College leaders have faced votes of no confidence for various reasons, including unpopular personnel decisions, financial management of the institution, or dismay with its direction. These votes do have some effect—recent investigations found that votes of no confidence that took place between 1989 and 2022 resulted in around half of the presidents leaving their jobs—a turnover of significant effect on campuses nationwide (Nietzel, 2023).

Votes of no confidence are a public and formal measure of expressing concern about leadership—and there are a variety of structures and rules about who can vote in these and how much of an effect such a vote can have. Neitzel (2023) noted that these types of votes tend to be symbolic in nature and more so a symptom of "chronic faculty unrest" (para. 9). There is more complexity to the issue of lack of confidence in leadership than solely the types of issues that lead to formal votes of no confidence. Those types of votes are rare and only include faculty in certain roles, not an entire representation of a campus. In a 2017 article published in the *Journal of Research on the College President,* the authors explored why campus leaders faced votes of "no confidence" from faculty bodies and how faculty perceived the role of such a vote. Votes of "no confidence" are unique to academia, and such votes signify the collective opinion that the faculty lacks confidence in a leader (Nadler et al., 2017, p. 25).

We approach this issue—the lack of confidence in leadership—as wider than a political statement. Instead, we investigate this issue in how it impacts any professional on campus and where other types of leadership missteps build the potential to create mistrust and dissatisfaction. It is possible that leaders may not know that they are laying the groundwork for others to lack trust in their decision-making.

WHAT HAPPENS WHEN WE LACK CONFIDENCE IN LEADERS?

Building a long-term career in education means you will likely meet and work for a variety of leaders. The American Council of Education (ACE) reports that the average tenure of a college president in 2023 was 5.9 years (a decrease over prior years) (Melidona et al.). Turnover within the various ranks of higher education likely follows a similar trend, with professionals entering and leaving the profession regularly, promotions causing movement into different roles, and turnover causing some disruption across campus.

One common assumption is that leaders should always be trusted. One condition we have noticed in our own work and in working with other professionals in higher education is that a lack of confidence in leadership can come on suddenly or grow over a longer period—and it can take place in a multitude of ways. Some leaders simply lack competence to do their jobs, which seems to create a logical reason for others to lack trust. Other leaders create patterns of inconsistent behaviors that, over time, cause others to lose trust in them. Others make such sudden mistakes or missteps that trust eviscerates quickly.

Specifically, professionals in higher education have shared examples of how blindly following leadership can take place. One professional shared that during an executive leadership change that took place on campus, a strategic plan that was underway was quietly removed from websites and never spoken of again. Another shared budget indiscretions by a campus leader that led to the leader's friends earning executive jobs on campus with no credentials to fill the roles. Several others told us about times their leader told them something and then turned around and did the complete opposite when carrying out a weighty decision. While we would like to embrace the notion that those in leadership positions unreservedly deserve respect and loyalty, most of us have lived through enough problems caused by poor leadership that we cannot ethically do so.

ACCIDENTAL LEADERS

Bad, effective, inefficient, and/or toxic leadership is not always something that we can blame on the leaders themselves, particularly in higher education. Organizational structures in higher education tend to be built with expertise from within; that is, many leadership roles are filled by promotion from within. However, step back and think about the training and education of many in higher education (faculty, practitioners, student services workers), and you might realize that very few of these professionals have leadership expertise. So, when a leadership role is earned or assigned, this person is learning on the job, often with little to no formal leadership training. Professor and author Vicki L. Baker writes about this phenomenon of promoting from within colleges and universities that "those individuals are promoted because of their tenure and knowledge about the institution—not because of their content knowledge, subject matter expertise or ability to set a vision and execute a strategy in that specific subject domain" (2023, para. 7). We call these professionals accidental leaders, not because they are prone to missteps but because, quite frequently, these individuals did not enter higher education with thoughts of moving into a department chair, dean, or administrative role. Many land in these roles by accident. We've met leaders in higher education who were appointed to department chair positions because they had taught the longest at the institution, deans who were appointed because they received high-ranking teaching awards, and even one administrator who said he landed his title because he happened to be the one answering the phone in the office the day the president called looking for someone to take on a leadership role.

Many enter leadership with little experience, but in higher education, there is little time to catch up or to receive formal leadership training, so most leaders learn their skills through trial and error on the job. This works out well for some, and yet it is disastrous for others. If we care about the quality of leadership in higher education, we should also care about the type and number of resources that are available to ensure leaders are prepared and competent to lead.

HOW LACK OF CONFIDENCE IN LEADERSHIP AFFECTS OUR SELF-CARE AND PROFESSIONAL STABILITY

When employees trust their leaders, there is less stress, more energy, higher productivity, more engagement, more satisfaction with their lives, and less burnout (Zak, 2017). On a personal level, this means an employee feels better about the organization, finds value and meaning in what they do, and may work harder for the greater good of that organization.

The erosion of trust increasingly convinces higher education professionals that their voices do not matter, that their work is expendable, and that they have no real control over their work. This type of condition weakens the morale of a workforce and produces dissent and dissatisfaction. Even with a change of leadership, these feelings and perceptions may not change, leaving a long-term impact on those who spend a great deal of their professional lives in the institution.

Also, lack of confidence creates instability in the leadership and the organization, which can leave a professional wondering if there is any security or sustainability within the organization. This may drive good employees to find work elsewhere or to leave higher education.

ACTIVITY: BUILDING TRUST FROM WITHIN

Confidence is built from within oneself, and trust is built within a team. Yet when a professional lacks confidence and then works in an environment where leaders may or may not be trustworthy, confidence erodes in all sorts of places. What matters in these conditions—where appointed leaders may be underqualified, where messaging may be confusing or conflicting, or where performance is unrecognized—is to maintain a clear resolve on your own confidence meter.

This two-part activity builds on psychologist Ron Friedman and IgnitePlus' research which surveyed 1,000 U.S.-based office workers to attempt to uncover the habits of high-performing teams. From that survey, the researchers found that around 8.7% of the 1,000 respondents had experienced high-performing teams (Friedman, 2025). Trust was an overarching theme among these high-performing teams, and as such, Friedman et al. suggested five behaviors that build trust. These behaviors are outlined in Part 1 of the next activity. As

Table 6.1 Behaviors That Build Trust to Support Professional Sustainability

Frequency of Behaviors That Build Trust		
Frequency You See These Behaviors in Others	Behaviors That Build Trust	Frequency You Recognize These Behaviors in Yourself
Always Sometimes Never	They do not leave collaboration to chance.	Always Sometimes Never
Always Sometimes Never	They keep colleagues in the loop.	Always Sometimes Never
Always Sometimes Never	They share credit.	Always Sometimes Never
Always Sometimes Never	They believe disagreements make them better.	Always Sometimes Never
Always Sometimes Never	They proactively address tension.	Always Sometimes Never

Source: Author created.

you read these behaviors, rank how often you experience them from two perspectives: (1) how you perceive your work with others, and (2) how you perceive yourself within that key area. Then in Step 2, below the ranking chart, use the space provided in Table 6.1 to describe how each of these behaviors can help you build trust and protect your own professional sustainability.

Part One: As you read the behaviors in the middle column, rank how often you experience these from two perspectives: (1) how you perceive your work with others, and (2) how you perceive yourself within that key area.

Part Two: Now that you have considered each of these behaviors that build trust, in the space provided here, reflect on how you can better build these behaviors. If few teams exhibit these trust-building conditions, what are you capable of, and which of these would make the most difference to you in helping you maintain your own self-care and professional sustainability?

CONCLUSION

Leadership is an element present in any professional role—whether you serve as the leader yourself or are stuck in the middle of leadership layers. Therefore, when we think strategically about self-care and professional sustainability, we consider not only the qualities that build trust in others but also how we can build capacity within ourselves to trust our own decision-making and work with others. The political nature of higher education will never change, so it is critical that we, as long-term professionals, think and behave in ways that build competence, both internally and externally. Recognizing the qualities that build trust among teams can help inform our own practices in ways that promote ethical decision-making and confidence in others for the duration of our professional lives.

REFLECTION QUESTIONS

1. How does it feel to lose trust in a colleague or leader? What experiences shape or form your ideas and feelings about trust?
2. Have you ever been assigned a leadership responsibility or role unexpectedly? How did this shape your internal confidence?
3. As a professional, why is being trusted by others important to you?
4. Think about your confidence levels in different professional settings. What tends to make your confidence strengthen or weaken? How can you recognize these moments in time so that you can control your confidence level better?
5. What are some things you can do differently now that you have considered confidence, trust, and professional sustainability?

CHAPTER 7

Delegation

WHY DO WE STRUGGLE WITH DELEGATION IN HIGHER EDUCATION?

When working in any professional community, including higher education, delegation seems to be one of the issues that challenges both leaders and followers alike. Nate Kreuter wrote about the aptitude of professionals in higher education in Inside Higher Education by stating, "I'm going to go way out on a limb and speculate that many of us in academe are bad delegators, perhaps not able to delegate responsibilities to others at all, or perhaps operating as micromanagers at those times when we do go ahead and delegate responsibilities to others" (2014, para. 1). It seems delegation does not come natural to most professionals for a variety of reasons: trust, time, perceived competence, and control, to name a few.

We bring up delegation as a topic related to building a self-care plan for a sustainable career in higher education because we know from personal experience that hosting an unwillingness to delegate can cause immense frustration and dissatisfaction, both on a personal and professional level.

WHY WE RESIST DELEGATION

There is a reason that delegation is considered both an art and a science—it requires not only thoughtful planning and consideration but also strategic decision-making when actually deciding to share one of your responsibilities with someone else. One of the reasons most professionals resist delegating tasks to others is the time that is lost in the process of explaining a duty. Imagine one of your responsibilities is to send a monthly department newsletter via email. You spend time each month generating content by sending requests for articles from your colleagues, seeking updates from campus outlets that may be of interest within your department, formatting the template, and ensuring the articles within are coherent. This task might take you 1 to 2 days total of smaller increments of time where you've emailed others, scanned news releases, and written content yourself. You know that an assistant could very well complete this job, but you are reluctant to explain the formatting, where you go to find information, or even how you manage the mailing list, so you continue to do this month after month.

Shifting the monthly mailing to your assistant is not a task that can be handed over easily, especially if you have set up norms that need to be maintained. However, step back and consider the task itself: one that you knowingly recognize is a time suck on your part and one that can, and probably should, be done by someone else. Table 7.1 shows there can be internal and external challenges to delegation. Recognizing you are holding on to tasks or responsibilities that could be done by others is the first step to recognizing that delegation is possible. But recognizing the possibility that you can delegate a task to someone else also presents some internal and external challenges to delegation itself:

1. **Teaching someone else to do a task will take time.** Learning to do the task took time. Sharing that work with someone else, explaining it, answering questions, and problem-solving for that employee will just take more time—and that's time you most likely do not have.
2. **You don't trust other people with your work.** More personally, you recognize that delegating one of your responsibilities to someone else is a reflection of you—your decision-making and leadership. This can create a sense of vulnerability on your part that can be quite unsettling.
3. **You fear losing control.** As a professional, you've earned your way to your position through hard work and dedication. Considering handing some of your responsibilities off to someone else can almost feel like you no longer matter or that you cannot control your career narrative.
4. **You worry about adding onto someone else's workload.** Delegating may lead to a feeling of guilt and like you are adding to the problem of an already overworked workplace.
5. **You want to be the expert.** You've earned your position because you know how to do it well. You are trusted by

Table 7.1 Internal and External Challenges to Delegation

Internal Challenges to Delegation	External Challenges to Delegation
Scared to let go of something known	Need to appear as the expert
Perceived incompetence of others	Already heavy workloads of others
Effort to train	Time to train
Losing control	Perception of incompetence
Don't know how	Lack of trust in others' abilities

Source: Author created.

leaders and colleagues, and not only did that take time, but it took intellectual and personal effort to build up a reputation as someone who knows what they are doing.

6. **You don't know how to delegate.** You know that delegation is more than just throwing a stack of files on someone's desk and telling them to "figure it out," even if that's how you were treated in your professional life. Perhaps you've never been delegated to effectively or you've never spent time planning how to best delegate to someone, so the thought of delegating seems overwhelming.

A CULTURE OF MISTRUST

For all of the various reasons we make excuses to not delegate, we know that being an effective delegator is a key part in building a sustainable career and professional life, particularly in higher education. It is not for a lack of caring or desire to delegate that we don't, but rather because we are often trained, through lived experiences, to be highly independent. For some, building a career in academia can be a lonely process. Many in higher education hold advanced degrees—working independently to become scholars, researchers, and teachers. In any role, they are expected to learn and know their field as an expert. This type of training (or lack thereof) can lead to a hyper-independence where you feel like you are the only person you can trust—that others are seeking to compete with you or undermine your decision-making.

Some of us are or lead nonacademic personnel—from staff, to student workers, to maintenance, to IT professionals. These roles are typically hired individuals who are skilled, knowledgeable, and willing to adapt and grow in a campus environment. However, they haven't experienced the cliques or customs of higher education, so there is an inherent learning curve that must be recognized.

Insert any of these types of people into a campus culture and the work conditions within higher education—long and overreaching working hours, expanding responsibilities, budget reductions, and political challenges—and the atmosphere itself seems unconducive to simply moving responsibilities off your own plate onto someone else's. And at times, we are implicitly or explicitly shamed for doing so. We are taught to be independent, to double-check our sources, to ensure our research methods are perfect, and to make only ethical decisions. This type of pressure, while not overtly present, is often used as veiled threats to end one's career—should you make a mistake, it is possible the institution would turn on you and you would lose your livelihood. This fear—of making a mistake, of misjudging someone's capacity to take on one of your responsibilities, or the potential for being seen as someone shirking duties—positions us to shun delegation rather than embrace it within leadership positions in higher education.

HOW LACK OF DELEGATION IMPACTS OUR SELF-CARE AND PROFESSIONAL SUSTAINABILITY

Housing an unwillingness to delegate a task because you fear losing control or think you don't have time to train someone else to do the job as good as you would creates an increasing workload of the unnecessary. That is, you insist that you continue to do tasks not because you want or need to, but because you think you cannot let go. Over time, this adds to our overall workload and can actually cause the quality of our work to decline, even though we kept the nondelegated task because we thought we were so good at it.

When we choose not to delegate, we continue to promote the narrative that we can do it all—work long hours, manage increasingly complex problems, lead others, and assume new responsibilities without time to do so. We affirm that not only are we the expert, but that we see ourselves as so important that no one else can be trusted to do our work—which, deep down, we know is not true. In a way, we are telling our leadership that their increasing demands and pressures are worth it to us regardless of the cost to our physical, personal, or mental well-being. We also waste time and effort that could be spent on more important things.

One piece that is often missed in delegation is gratitude. Whether you are delegating or being delegated to, a human element of gratitude for sharing a task, learning something new, or being open to teaching someone new knowledge should not go unnoticed or unspoken—yet it does. We often pass tasks on to each other's plates without a recognition for the effort undertaken or the quality of the work presented. We cover our inability to be gracious with a workplace persona of "taking one for the team," which, over time, can erode trust and goodwill. Failing to demonstrate gratitude erodes confidence and willingness to take risks, which, in turn, can build resentment.

Beyond an increased workload, we miss some amazing opportunities to build others up. In your own career, you were most likely delegated a task or two along the way. Think about how learning those new skills enhanced your professional life. Some of these may not have been glamorous, but over time, you learned to manage and grow from being trusted to do something new. Delegating is not only just about you, but it is also about growing others, and by delegating, you are not only expanding their skill set but are demonstrating a belief in their ability and future in the institution. This type of affirmation costs nothing and yet can promote a positive affinity for the organization, even without financial reward.

Leaders who delegate are more efficient and future driven. A 2014 study by Gallup found that among entrepreneurs, those who delegate are able to accomplish more, push their ideas further, and create new opportunities more rapidly. Leadership and communication consultant David Grossman (2023), when exploring the findings of Gallup's survey, stated:

> Although delegation is critical to a company's success, managers also need to remember that it's not about just pushing off the boring or difficult jobs on others. It's also important to understand that when delegating, leaders should provide consistent support yet with some autonomy, so employees still feel entrusted and empowered to do the work creatively or to suggest new or better ways of achieving the outcomes. (para. 10)

Strong leaders, including those within any level of higher education, understand the capacity for their own talent and time and also recognize the responsibility to delegate to others in order to promote professional competency, but also to spend their time on more important things like growth, innovation, and quality management. These leaders recognize that their drive for independence or autonomy should not rule the sensibility of shared responsibility.

REVEALING THE SECRET OF FREEDOM

Delegation, it seems, takes planning, thought, and input. Our recommendation in this chapter is to think about tasks, responsibilities, or things in your life of which you might be able to let go. But before you begin that brainstorming process, we'd like to reveal a wonderful outcome of delegation: freedom. Effectively delegating (and, yes, this includes the training of someone else to do the task, communicating frequently to answer questions and offer advice, and trusting them to do well) can provide you the time and space you need to accomplish even greater things. You can now step outside your box of busyness and venture into dreaming big. You might be able to refine a process that you know has been broken for years or to forge a partnership with a local business you've been meaning to meet with. You might connect more frequently with alumni or design new learning opportunities within the institution. The point here is not that you fill that time back up, but that you fill that time up with things that light your passion, that remind you of why you work in academia, and that reward you for your ingenuity and creativity.

DELEGATION DETERMINATION

As a higher education professional, it is important to recognize that you can't do everything on your own and maintain a healthy work–life balance. As you progress in your career, you may find a time that the number of tasks on your to-do list begins to outweigh the amount of time in your workday. This should be an indicator that you may need to find other ways to complete tasks that support the critical work of your program, department, or institution. In the short term, you may have enough energy and stamina to complete the work that needs to be done, but over time the strain will begin to weigh on your productivity. By managing workload effectively and delegating, leaders can achieve a better work–life balance, reduce stress, keep burnout at bay, and enhance professional sustainability.

According to the Society for Human Resources Management, leaders should establish a delegation attitude (Lloyd, 2024). As your to-do list increases and the completed check marks decrease, you should ask yourself, "Who else could complete this task?" As a leader, you should question every task you complete, particularly those you have done for years, to determine if there are others in your program, department, or institution that could grow professionally by learning new skills (Lloyd, 2024).

The three-step activity that we've adapted from the Task-Delegation Worksheet from the website Teach Better.com is a "Delegation Blueprint" of sorts. This will assist you in observing and documenting what tasks you complete throughout a typical workweek and consider if you enjoy, dislike, struggle, or never have time to complete them. Then you will reflect on the results of your data collection to help determine which tasks would be easiest to delegate, which would be hardest to delegate, and which would save you the most time if you delegated them to someone else (Progressive Mastery Learning, 2025).

As you complete the Delegation Blueprint activity, it is important to be detailed and honest. It will be hard to determine what tasks are contenders for delegation if you don't have an accurate account of what you spend your time doing in a typical workweek. Another approach to complete the activity is to consider a busy time of year for your role, such as the beginning of a semester, the end of the semester, or the fiscal year-end. You can reflect on those critical times in your position and complete the Delegation Blueprint with that time period in mind.

ACTIVITY: DELEGATION BLUEPRINT

Step One: Observation

Create a document similar to Table 7.2 to observe and document what tasks you complete over the next workweek. You can create the tracking document on your phone, in a word processing application on your computer, or with pen and paper. The tasks you document should accurately represent your current workload, ranging from big to small tasks, from scheduling a meeting to writing a new administrative policy. If you complete the task multiple times, make a tally mark next to it to provide perspective on how often you complete the task.

Table 7.2 Personal Assessment of Task Enjoyment

Task	Enjoy You look forward to completing these tasks.	Dislike You dread completing these tasks.	Struggle You don't dread these tasks, BUT you're not good at them.	Never Have Time You want to complete these tasks BUT never have time.

Source: Progressive Mastery Learning (2025).

Step Two: Review and Reflect

- What surprised you about the tasks that ended up in each of the columns?
- Why do the tasks in the Enjoy column bring you satisfaction?
- Reflecting on the dislike, struggle, and never have time columns, what emotions do you feel about those tasks?

Step Three: Identify and Delegate

After reviewing the columns and reflection questions in the previous section, what tasks would you like to delegate? List them in the Task column in Table 7.3. Then share the potential challenges in the other column in Table 7.3. This might include emotional barriers or feelings that you associate with delegating this task, such as guilt, lack of trust, fear of losing control, perfectionism, fear of burdening others, time constraints associated with training, lack of delegation skills, or worry of what others might think about delegating the task.

Based on the tasks you listed in Table 7.3:

- Circle the top three tasks you would like to delegate.
- Write the letter "E" by the task that would be easiest to delegate.
- Write the letter "H" by the task that would be hardest to delegate.

Table 7.3 Identifying Challenges to Delegation of Identified Tasks

Task	Potential Challenges With Delegating
1.	
2.	
3	
4.	
5.	
6.	

- Write the letter "T" by the task that would save you the most time if you delegated it to someone else.
- Based on this information, what is one task that you will delegate?

Now that you have identified one task that you plan to delegate, you need to prepare an action plan to begin that process. It is important to prepare for the conversations that need to take place for a successful transition. As you prepare for the transfer of responsibilities, remember that delegation is a shared opportunity for you and the person receiving the new task or responsibility. You will have more time to focus on critical issues and tasks that will move the program, department, or institution forward. The employee will have the opportunity to grow and develop through completing new tasks. What follows is a Delegation Checklist to ensure that all the details are addressed.

DELEGATION CHECKLIST

- ☐ Alert the proper campus contacts about what task you are planning to delegate, who will be acquiring the task, and an overview of the transition plan. You want to ensure that all the proper leadership positions are aware of the upcoming change. Ask them to refrain from sharing the news until you have an opportunity to speak with the person acquiring the delegated task.
- ☐ Schedule a time to meet with the person who will be acquiring the delegated assignment.
- ☐ Start the meeting by sharing why you have selected them to acquire the task.

- ❑ Ask them if they are willing to take on the new task.
    - ❑ If they agree, proceed with the next step on the checklist.
    - ❑ If they decline the opportunity, discuss their reason for not wanting to acquire the new task.
- ❑ Provide a detailed overview of what the task includes.
- ❑ Inform them about the resources available on campus to assist in successfully completing the new task (budget, faculty/staff, equipment, materials, etc.).
- ❑ Confirm the person's understanding of and commitment to the new task. This is a common failure in delegation discussions.
- ❑ After the meeting, inform others who need to know about the delegated assignment.
- ❑ Establish a regular check-in plan while the person is learning how to complete the new task. Make sure to provide both constructive and regular feedback at the check-in meetings.
- ❑ Be accessible for questions as the person is learning the new task. Establish what this might look like: a Zoom call, an email, or an open door policy to stop by as needed.
- ❑ Once the task is completed for the first time, review the results or outcomes. Provide constructive feedback.
- ❑ Reflect with the person about lessons learned and how they will approach the task next time.

Now that you have identified what task can be delegated and reviewed how to create a successful transition plan, respond to the following question: What will you do with the extra time the delegated task took to complete?

CONCLUSION

Delegation can be a higher education professional's best friend or worst enemy. Learn to delegate well, and you will free up time to do amazing and wonderfully creative things. Delegate poorly, and you can get stuck in a trend of micromanagement and frustration. Instead of using delegation only as a means of giving away tasks you do not enjoy, strategizing how and when to delegate can protect your valuable time. Additionally, it can be an investment in someone else—someone you can help grow as a professional and someone who might find new and innovative ways to complete those tasks you used to dread. Delegation takes time and hosts a necessity to provide feedback, but when done well, delegation can create conditions for a more balanced and fulfilling professional life.

REFLECTION QUESTIONS

1. Think about your own experience being delegated to—how did it make you feel, and what did you learn from the experience?
2. What challenges do you face in delegating tasks to others? How might you overcome these challenges?
3. If you were able to delegate a few tasks to someone trusted, what would you do with that open time and space?
4. How might your organization create better routines of delegation so that it is expected rather than avoided?
5. What are some things you can do differently now that you've considered communication and your professional sustainability?

CHAPTER 8

Professional Stagnation and the Need for Individualized Growth Options

WHY DO WE STRUGGLE WITH PROFESSIONAL DEVELOPMENT OFFERINGS IN HIGHER EDUCATION?

Professional growth and development within a higher education setting should be an expectation of all, in that, there should be an exchange of needs and desires both from the professional and from the institution. The professional seeks to gain knowledge, new insights and information, feedback, and practice through collaborative learning, while the institution can better align its professionals around strategic planning, institutional goals, and collaborative input. It is really a give and take—both sides have something to give (knowledge, lived experiences, opinions), and both have something they seek to get (insider expertise, on-the-ground information, and increased professional aptitude of the professionals in the institution).

Professor and author Robin Middlehurst pointed at specific areas regarding the unique needs of professionals working in higher education, including faculty, staff, and other administrative personnel. These considerations included (1) the kind of education professionals needed in the future, (2) the kinds of developmental opportunities that would promote growth of professional skills and identity, (3) the "capabilities and capacities" needed to be developed to grow as a higher education professional, and (4) the future potential to utilize these "capabilities and capacities" (Middlehurst, 2009, p. 223). In short, working in higher education does not dispose one of inherent professional growth and development opportunities.

GROWTH DOES NOT OCCUR WITHOUT INTENTION

Working long-term in higher education has exposed us to various attempts by institutions and people within those institutions to promote professional development and growth—some successful, some not. These include mandatory online training, day-long workshops, retreats, and conferences. Some of these were extraordinarily helpful and educational, whereas others were not. When it comes to professional growth and development within the academy, it is often a haphazard approach. Depending on your leader, available funds, and emerging needs, the variety and approach to professional offerings can be sporadic and disconnected.

One thing remains clear: true professional development and growth are really left up to you. No one will carefully monitor your growth and ask you what opportunities you think would best fit your career path or would help the institution the most. It is possible, we believe, to have a lifelong career in higher education without ever being pushed to become a better teacher, leader, or professional through professional growth opportunities. If this is the case, we are often left making up the script as we go—finding opportunities that best match our interests, sometimes paying for those opportunities ourselves, and rarely having any follow-up on the capabilities or capacities homed in on during that development.

Professional development need not be formal. We acknowledge that much of it is inherent to the work that we do, to the leaders that we learn from along the way, and from lived experiences. Professional development need not be expensive—some of the best learning we have experienced has been sitting around a lunch table or assisting a student through a complex research problem. However, the assumption is typically made that if you are going to grow as a professional, it is up to you to manage.

CHANGING NEEDS FOR PROFESSIONAL DEVELOPMENT

If we hope or plan to work in higher education in any capacity over time, professional development should be a professional habit. Because we know change is frequent, the needs and demands placed on institutions are constantly in flux, and our roles within institutions tend to evolve and overlap as we experience job creep and additional responsibilities. We need the chance to fine-tune our skills to the current day.

Even if an institution offers professional development opportunities, it is often through a one-size-fits-all approach. Consider a department that sponsors a diversity-education speaker to help an enrollment management office better understand ways to recruit more culturally and economically diverse students. The entire department sits in a conference room, including the department leader, admissions personnel, and front-office staff. They all receive the same training, hear the same points about student recruiting, and leave with a similar experience. While each brings their own lived experiences to the table, the offering itself was not personal to the individuals attending.

Professional development should be an individualized and built-in partnership with each professional throughout their career. That is, a conversation of some sort, whether formal or informal, whether within performance evaluations or outside, that provides a space for the professional to express their goals and interests should be purposeful and regular. In this same space, there should be feedback to help the professional better understand areas of growth that might be beneficial.

We turned to some experts in professional development for K–12 educators, Linda Darling-Hammond, Maria Hyler, and Madelyn Gardner (2017), who laid out eight elements of effective professional development. In our application to higher education settings, these include:

- Being content focused: think beyond one's content area for teaching and focus on the content (roles, duties, responsibilities) that are learned and developed over time.
- Incorporating active learning: in higher education, this would be more than sit-and-get seminars or Zoom learning sessions. Engaging and meaningful learning opportunities that focus specifically on professional growth should embrace adult learning methods.
- Supporting collaboration: while professional development should be individualized to one's needs throughout her career, this endeavor should not be done in isolation and should build meaningful connections that promote shared growth.
- Using models of effective practice: growth opportunities should be purposeful and designed to suit the individual—and in a way that complements the institution.
- Providing coaching and support: professional growth should not occur in a vacuum and should welcome engagement from colleagues.

- Providing space for reflection and feedback: this includes purposeful time to consider one's professional standing, desired growth areas, and direction on how reflection can promote self-awareness.
- Extending for a sustained duration: a long-term commitment from the professional and the institution to invest in growth, learning, and development is necessary.

You will notice that we are not discussing professional development and growth in this chapter as a means of reprimand, but rather to invest in and recognize that as professionals, we change over time. The professional development sessions we needed and wanted to attend as new faculty changed as we spent more time in the academy. Our own needs and interests shifted from best practices in teaching to better understanding how to lead others and how to help others build a career path that the institution could support. We also sought out ways to innovate technology in our classrooms and workspaces and how to understand the ever-changing needs of employers hiring our students.

HOW PROFESSIONAL DEVELOPMENT IMPACTS OUR SELF-CARE AND LONG-TERM PROFESSIONAL SUSTAINABILITY

Professional growth does not happen by accident. In the middle of busy days, demanding semesters, multitudes of students, and changing environments, it may seem like professional growth in higher education is inevitable—and it might be in some cases. However, it is known that as educators move through their careers, their needs for personalized professional development growth options, often self-directed ones, are the ones that are the most impactful. In this, one-sized-fits-all approaches seem impersonal and repetitive. Yet what we see in terms of professional growth options in higher education are usually found in two arenas: trainings or self-directed professional design. Training tends to consist of requirements such as compliance sessions on federal regulations or mandated training on workplace practices. Author Tami Meyer suggested training is a way for organizations to fill present gaps, while professional development is focused on future growth (2023).

When professionals are invited to participate in designing professional growth planning with the institution, there can be a mutual benefit. The professional feels their talents matter, and the institution can tailor growth that benefits needs at the institution. This match creates a healthy recognition that each needs the other and that their interests in the future can be codesigned. Meyer consulted with professional growth coach Steve Smith in 2023, noting the ways that professional development benefits the professional receiving it. These include:

- Staying relevant: It encourages and allows the employee to stay up to date on emerging issues, trends in education, and nuances in organizational change. This empowers professionals and helps them feel valued and knowledgeable within the organization. As a result, there is a greater chance the professional will feel rewarded and invested in their career.
- Professional satisfaction: Ongoing meaningful learning boosts confidence and a feeling of purpose in work.
- Meaningful recognition: An investment in professional development demonstrates an interest in keeping an employee, which boosts retention and a willingness to stay for a longer period.

The business of higher education is centered around learning processes, so it is a natural connection to encourage and support professional development to retain talented professionals who can help fulfill the organization's mission.

ACTIVITY: CREATING YOUR OWN PROFESSIONAL GROWTH PLAN

Professional development opportunities should be personalized and developed in concert between an organization and the professional working within that organization. That is, an organization, like a college or university, should not demand a one-size-fits-all professional development approach for all professionals, nor should professionals seek professional development opportunities that offer no benefit to the organization. This should be a mutually beneficial arrangement, yet one that recognizes the various interests, professional aspirations, and individuality of the professional.

Where does self-care fit within a professional growth plan? It should be present throughout because they are so intertwined. When

Table 8.1 Professional Growth Plan

Professional Growth Plan	Professional Area of Growth: ______	Professional Area of Growth: ______	Professional Area of Growth: ______
Plan: Draft your goal statement (a concise statement about how you would like to grow)			
Learn: Resources to consider (books, conferences, people, etc.)			
Implement: When/where can you implement what you have learned?			
Balance: How does this action promote/impact self-care?			
Recognize: What do I hope my overall growth will be?			

Source: Author created.

self-care is ignored, professional growth lags. When professional growth lags, so do motivation and desire for meaningful self-care. Thus, the professional growth plan you design later will incorporate both. In Table 8.1, identify two or three areas in which you would like to grow professionally. Then brainstorm in the boxes provided what steps you need to take by considering the overarching goal, what resources you will need, how you will implement what you have learned, how this area of growth will positively impact your self-care, and how you will recognize that the goal has been met and growth occurred.

CONCLUSION

Professional development and growth are more than a series of trainings or courses that one takes during a career. Professional growth, ideally, should be individualized as a professional grows and evolves—recognizing that lived experiences, knowledge gained, and professional relationships all inform and change how a professional seeks to grow and evolve. Professional growth should not be considered apart from self-care, as each is integral to the other. Instead, professionals should consider in what areas they wish to grow, how those areas align with organizational needs and goals, and how self-care practices can be built and sustained with the new knowledge. As professionals, we should encourage and model this to others—showing that professional growth will be a journey unique to the individual and one that complements an investment in long-term professional development that benefits both the individual and the organization.

REFLECTION QUESTIONS

1. How does my current role in higher education support my long-term career aspirations, and what additional opportunities can I pursue to work toward my goals?
2. What challenges or barriers to professional growth might I encounter, and how can I overcome these obstacles to continue growing?
3. How can I balance my current role and responsibilities with my long-term professional aspirations, ensuring that both my current and future career goals are met when I shut my office door on campus for the last time?
4. Where will I post or place my professional growth plan to keep my career aspirations present in my everyday activities?
5. Who will I share my professional growth plan with to hold me accountable for the steps that I need to complete to ensure that I continue to work toward my career aspirations?

CHAPTER 9

"Job Creep" and High-Achieving Professionals

WHY DO WE STRUGGLE WITH OUR INCREASINGLY DEMANDING WORKLOAD?

The workload in higher education, for any position, can be untenable and even unmanageable. Leading in these settings can absolutely be the result of lack of control or lack of job clarity, but it is important to consider workload in and of itself. When thinking about your job, you may think of the wide list of responsibilities you hold—from accountability measures, to communication responsibilities, to supervision and work alongside others. The type of work that you do can cause a unique type of stress—higher education jobs are often intellectual in nature, require an advanced degree to move up professionally, and require reflection and self-awareness. Over time, working in a demanding academic environment or advocating for an unpopular agenda can tax your mental and physical resources. Yet what is it about workload, in and of itself, that challenges our self-care in ways different from jobs outside of higher education?

One facet of the workload that is difficult to manage is the unpredictability of the work itself. Standing aside role clarity, professionals in higher education are working in a setting unlike many others—built around intellectual personalities, among structures that can go back decades in time, and around policies that remain difficult to change. These facets of what seems to be stability can also provide substantive instability—or assuming roles that go unnoticed or unrecognized.

The unmanageable and unpredictable workloads seem to be the result of "job creep"—or the inevitable nature of a job where if you do your job well, you will likely have more to do. By building trust, demonstrating competence, and adhering to expected customs and norms, you begin to "fit" into the world of academia.

"JOB CREEP" AND THE UNMANAGEABLE OR UNPREDICTABLE WORKLOAD

If you are like us, you accept additional responsibilities with a willing spirit. Being trusted with additional roles or tasks generally means you're being rewarded for being not only a strong employee but one with a strong work ethic as well. Van Dyne and Ellis (2004) coined the term "job creep" to refer to situations in which employees "feel ongoing pressure to do more than the requirements of their jobs" (p. 181). In higher education, these additional responsibilities can seem like honors or recognition, when, in reality, they add to the already difficult load of the original job. Some subtle ways these responsibilities start piling onto your job duties might include:

- Increasing your teaching load, whether for additional pay or not. The increase in pay may account for some of the work required, but may not account for the time lost that was needed to further your research path or complete your administrative work.
- Managing multiple teaching environments, including remote, in-person, and hybrid/multiple work options. While the influx of a variety of work possibilities has provided more flexibility to a traditional workday, the multiple options of ways to work can also cause overlap—teaching multiple sections of courses in both face-to-face and online settings, meeting with colleagues both online and in conference rooms, or collaborating with others beyond work hours.
- Assuming responsibility for complex projects with similar deadlines can go unnoticed if you are the "go-to" person for a certain task, yet, year to year, as your role changes and you are assigned other responsibilities and managing new processes, that complex problem can become a complex time-consuming problem that you no longer have time to devote to and ensure its success.
- Loss of staff and faculty lines shifts responsibilities immediately onto others with little time to waste. Tasks that were once assigned to a role are split, shifted, modified, and assigned to others, many times without any consideration or thoughtful approach to current workload.
- Controlling the perceived need to be responsive during nonworking hours. Technology is one of the key perpetrators

> of unmanageable and unpredictable workloads, mostly because it avails you of a 24/7 work schedule. Without clear boundaries, emails are sent and received during late evening or early morning times, response times become increasingly shorter, and the ability to distance oneself from work is increasingly difficult. Technology does increase the speed for how many jobs can be done, but because of that, it can also increase the amount of work that is expected to be done in the same time span, thus increasing responsibilities.

Scholar Dr. Jenna Mittelmeier describes the glorification of overwork in higher education. She stated in a 2023 blog post, "Academia has a culture that valorizes feeling perpetually overburdened and fatigued. This, of course, manifests in structural ways through precariousness, unmanageable workloads, inequalities, and bullying" (para. 4). Through her studies, she noticed that in higher education, employees are often shamed for not participating in the overwork culture. She noted that employees are often praised for working during leave or responding to emails during nonwork hours—thus, creating a toxic atmosphere where working traditional hours is considered underperforming and, in some ways, disloyal.

BEING A HIGH-ACHIEVING LEADER IN HIGHER EDUCATION

Seeking to perform as a high-achieving professional in higher education can be like a roller coaster: both exhilarating and terrifying all at the same time. On one hand, you are exceptional at managing multiple tasks at once. Your professional products stand above the rest. You hit milestones for being one of the most dedicated people in your department. On the other hand, those same traits that cause you to excel, put in extra hours, and strive for your next promotion are also your greatest detriment; that is, you work to exhaustion, you sacrifice meaningful relationships in exchange for short-term goals, and you see failure as a personal shortcoming.

The problem facing high achievers is that it is difficult to limit it to just one aspect of your life. That is, while striving to be a high achiever in your professional life, your personal life takes a toll and vice versa. Although it is possible to find a balance, at times, that need to push for more success and accomplishments often causes you to take detours that you view as temporary pit stops or momentary steps off a given path. In essence, being a high achiever means that balance is not a strength. However, high achievers are also the most prone to suffer from burnout (Freudenberger & Richelson, 1980). That is, for all the dedication and time spent investing in becoming an exceptional leader, there is also a cost—and that cost may come in the form of being overwhelmed, tired, and suffering from burnout.

Move this into today's higher education landscape, and the problems compound. Professionals in higher education, including leaders at all levels and positions—those known for helping, working long hours, handling adversity from hour to hour—are some of our most talented campus contributors. They have demonstrated a dedication to their jobs, unlike any others—and as a society, we've come to expect a certain amount of sacrifice from these high performers. For many of us, it is common to expect a colleague to return our phone call within a reasonable time or to be present at numerous events outside of the regular workday. The highly recruited and praised workaholic higher education leader is also at the greatest risk for burnout, particularly because colleges and universities rarely, if ever, invest resources into the care and well-being of their own leaders.

Instead, for all the same reasons that society praises high achievers for their accomplishments, dedication, and work ethic, the high achievers, including those within our campuses, also invoke temporary measures to protect their short-term well-being and sanity. In fact, being a high achiever of success also means being an equally high achiever at employing coping mechanisms to make up for one's shortcomings, weaknesses, or emotional trials. That is, being a high achiever is not limited solely to your professional or personal accomplishments—it also encompasses how you adjust to and address life's challenges and tribulations. As a high achiever, you tend to practice those same traits—excessive ambition, extraordinary drive, and a willingness to sacrifice—as you both excel and spiral into self-destruction.

ASSUMPTIONS ABOUT THE HIGH-ACHIEVING PROFESSIONAL

Leaders in higher education emerge through a variety of pathways, circumstances, and avenues. Considering educational venues in particular, it makes sense that many former high-achieving students then move into academic leadership roles at all levels—after all, it's a setting where we've had success in the past. As students, the goal was to make the "A" honor roll or a perfect score on a test. However, high-achieving professionals in higher education tend to exhibit some similar tendencies in how they approach their academic careers. Consider some of the most common traits of high-achieving professionals:

1. **Working harder, not smarter:** High achievers put in extra hours, focus on tasks more closely than others, and are focused on the outcome. As such, high achievers will often be the ones that leaders turn to when a critical problem arises or a task must be accomplished by a deadline. The high achiever will go above and beyond to find success and believes that hard work creates a direct path to success.
2. **Always powered "on":** High achievers stay focused on a given task. They can finely tune their ideas to achieve an intended outcome. They often work longer hours, forego meals and social events, and believe that dedication will lead to greater things. In higher education, these are the people working late, burning the midnight oil, and making progress on their to-do list over the weekend.
3. **Never says no:** Most leaders utilize the "yes" members of their team for obvious reasons—they are agreeable and willing to take on additional work. Furthermore, these high achievers will overbook, rearrange, or change plans to meet the needs of others. In higher education, this may look like serving on multiple committees, volunteering to take on additional roles or titles without compensation, or feeling compelled to offer a hand to a colleague in need.
4. **Gold-medal ambition:** Creating goals is a positive approach to track achievements, but the high achiever never stops once a goal is achieved. What this means is that when one goal is achieved, another one is on the horizon. The high achiever rarely takes the time to recognize and celebrate when a goal is achieved. For example, faculty aspire to become associate deans who then work diligently to become "full deans." Achieving that next step then leads to a yearning for the one after that, and so on and so on.
5. **Architect of chaos:** Structure and purpose keep the high achiever focused, but life isn't always amenable to this type of blueprint. One way to focus is through meticulous organizational tactics, from planning to output. They do not have time to allow disorganization to interfere with their goal-centeredness, so it is quite likely the high achiever has a

structured routine and method of keeping ideas and things in an orderly fashion. Many high-achieving leaders utilize sticky notes to excess, manage one (or more) online calendars, and are rarely late to appointments.

6. **Scientist of smart:** Acquiring new skills and having an inquisitive nature is common to high achievers. That is, given a new task, the high achiever will adapt and learn how to do new things to accomplish it. Educators as learners often read professional books for pleasure (or have no desire to read for pleasure) and spend time on pursuits that will enhance their professional goals. You'll often see these leaders seeking out mentors, attending professional development centered on leadership growth, and building networking opportunities within the field.
7. **An influencer status:** Starting at a young age, high achievers are groomed to find success within the fruits of their hard work. Hard work leads to accomplishments. Accomplishments lead to recognition. Recognition leads to elevated status and more responsibility. For leaders in higher education, this may mean earning teaching accolades and awards, exceptional performance reviews, and publicity from within the campus and the local community.

As you reflect on the list of traits of high-achieving professionals on campus, you may notice that these are all desirable traits in some form or another. That is, higher education professionals want to hire and/or be ambitious, goal-oriented people. We also want our leaders to be high achievers. Additionally, having the confidence that the high-achieving professional will meet any goal put in front of them means the likelihood of reward to the leader is also magnified.

Take a closer look at these tendencies. Notice that each has a tipping point, where something very positive, like hard work, can become destructive; for example, hard work that directly causes physical or mental illness over time. Or consider how one's ambition might cause collegial coworkers to begin to feel competitive in nature, resulting in one undermining the work of another. Tendencies are just that—traits that "tend" to happen like a seesaw (see Figure 9.1), where extra pressure on one side can lead to a desirable result, but redundant pressure on the other end leads to a completely undesirable outcome.

Figure 9.1 Balancing high-achieving traits.

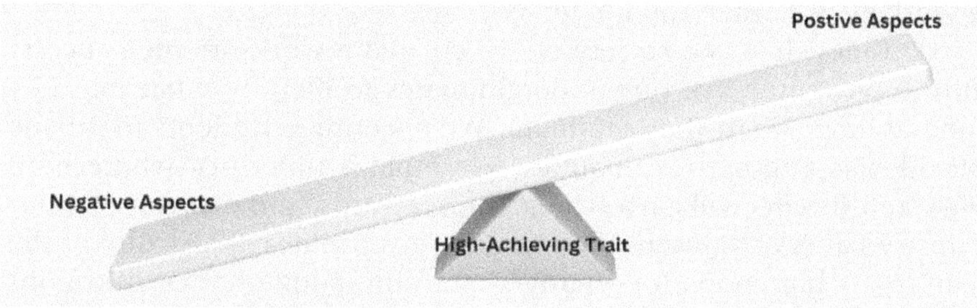

Source: Created by Gretchen Oltman.

HOW JOB CREEP AND HIGH-ACHIEVING TRAITS IMPACT OUR SELF-CARE AND PROFESSIONAL SUSTAINABILITY

For as much praise as high-achieving professionals are likely to receive for meeting goals and success-driven outcomes on today's campuses, they also likely have the battle scars caused by their journey. It's not so much that high achievers are halted by injuries or obstacles—after all, they are known for their capability of finding workarounds and ways to succeed when others cannot. They also maintain the tendency to be able to find temporary fixes for the obstacles that cause them short-term distress. High achievers excel at finding ways to hide, cover, or disguise their problems in the same way that they meet goals, work ambitiously, and accomplish great things—with extreme precision and skill.

Living and working as a high achiever can lead to a highly destructive lifestyle—addiction, illness, and turmoil. What we imagine as the accomplishments of the high achiever—publication, fame, success, glory—also hides the mechanisms high achievers use to cover their flaws. Also hidden within these fleeting moments is the need to produce more perfection. That is, as goal-oriented individuals, once a goal is reached, the high achiever spends very little time enjoying the met goal and moves onto creating a new goal and resetting a pace for more achievement. What was once enough is now not enough and more must be attained.

Within the aura of hard work and dedication also creeps in the lingering self-doubt often present with a high achiever. Questions begin to arise: What if I'm not good enough? What if I fail? What if I look stupid? These questions roll around in one's mind, pushing back against achievements earned and, in turn, pushing the high achiever to work even harder and longer.

Consider that as a society we've created a work-oriented success culture. We often ask our undergraduates to identify what job they hope to have when they graduate. We encourage students to pursue job titles as opposed to qualities. We build a trajectory where hard work and success will earn scholarships, awards, and recognition. Our industry papers are littered with numerous profiles of "Faculty of the Year" or "Champions for Change." Earning additional certifications creates more and higher-paying job opportunities. Attaining promotion or tenure secures one's status as a stable campus entity. Staying long-term on the college campus, perhaps for the duration of one's career, can suggest a waning work ethic or a lack of desire to advance professionally—all of which is contrary to what our campuses need the most: qualified, energetic, and innovative academics.

Being a high-achieving professional is hard, but being a high achiever in a higher educational setting—where much of our time is spent on goal setting, watching others grow and learn, and measuring progress through sometimes arbitrary means—is one of the darkest places to be. Added to the complexity of self-sabotage and self-judgment is the competing desire to help and serve people. That is, most in higher education have some sort of "helping" gene wherein their passion for their jobs comes from the ability to teach, change, and inspire the lives of others. This constant desire to be present and give up time for others in turn means there is less time for personal care and well-being. In fact, the high-achieving professional will often sacrifice personal time, time with family and friends, and self-care time to get that last stack of paper graded, to answer the list of incoming emails, or to attend a campus function. Burnout makes one of our most promising institutions one of the most difficult to live within for the high-achieving professional.

ACTIVITY: BALANCING YOUR HIGH-ACHIEVING TRAITS SEESAW

Recall the idea that we are all balancing our high-achieving traits and our increasing workload simultaneously. This can cause our professional and personal lives to become easily unbalanced in favor of unsustainable patterns or unhealthy choices. In Table 9.1, you'll find the

Table 9.1 Personal Assumptions and Attributes of High-Achieving Traits

Positive Aspects of This Trait	Assumptions About the High Achiever	Negative Aspects of This Trait
	Working smarter, not harder	
	Always powered on	
	Never say no	
	Gold-medal ambition	
	Architect of chaos	
	Scientist of smart	
	Influencer status	

Source: Author created.

assumptions that are made about high-achieving workers in the midst of increasing workload. Reflect on your professional life and think about times when you've exhibited each trait. Then, on both sides of the identified trait, list positive and negative aspects of said trait—how that trait might both benefit you and potentially harm your self-care and professional sustainability.

CONCLUSION

Workload, job creep, stress, burnout, and high-achieving tendencies of professionals in higher education tend to all go hand in hand, which is why we have not isolated these, but rather combined them into a gentle concert of human conditions within this chapter. As a professional, if you work long hours to complete a project, there will be a natural result of something else being out of balance in your life (rest, family time, completion of other job responsibilities, etc.). Work–life balance is something that every professional wrestles with, but what we've found to be more applicable in higher education is to recognize that work–life balance is constantly a tension—even the most accomplished professionals are constantly balancing and rebalancing their seesaw of traits and responsibilities. In this, the most important element is recognizing when your desire for achievement is negatively impacting your quality of life—a clear symptom that your seesaw needs to be rebalanced to something that can help build your professional sustainability.

REFLECTION QUESTIONS

1. Think about your work–life balance today. Where is there room for improvement and where do you struggle to maintain a balance? Why is this?
2. What pieces of your current role are a result of increasing responsibilities or job creep? How have you integrated those into your professional duties and rebalanced your work–life condition?
3. Is job creep infiltrating your campus? How might you articulate a case to pause and recognize when duties are being redistributed or responsibilities are quietly expanding to bring notice to this?
4. What would the ideal work–life balance look like to you? What are some steps you can take to move toward that ideal?
5. What are some things you can do differently now that you've considered job creep, workload, and high-achieving professional traits?

CHAPTER 10

Creating Your Self-Care Plan for Professional Sustainability

HOW DO WE DO IT ALL?

Self-care is an essential skill for higher education professionals (King-White & Rogers, 2018). According to Miller et al. (2018), "Faculty engaging in self-care can have the exponential impact of more sustained professional engagement. This sustained engagement through effective self-care can benefit students, faculty, universities, and the profession itself" (p. 1056). Thus, developing a self-care plan can support professional sustainability and define not only what you hope to accomplish but the type of professional you want to be throughout your career in higher education. A self-care plan can map out what you want to achieve in both the short term and long term, meaning it is more than an evaluative moment in time, but rather a purposeful investment in your professional future. Additionally, a well-developed self-care plan can serve as a valuable guide, helping you navigate the ups and downs of your career in higher education. Dedication and loyalty alone will not lead to professional sustainability if your self-care practices have not been addressed. Here are several reasons why it is imperative that professionals in higher education create a self-care plan for sustainability:

1. A self-care plan provides a framework for professionals to be more **intentional** about the direction of their career. For instance, knowing that you want to continue your career in higher education, a self-care plan can provide you with a North Star or moral compass to follow in times of uncertainty.
2. A well written self-care plan can put setbacks or accomplishments into **perspective** and allow you to see the bigger picture of your career—in a sense, reminding you that your career is a marathon, not the 100-meter dash.

3. Having an actionable self-care plan makes you more **resilient** when things do not go your way. It allows you to move forward after facing adversity so that professional challenges do not feel like they are taking over your entire personal and professional life.
4. Professional sustainability self-care plans help you **acknowledge** what skills you need to maintain and develop to remain an effective member of the academy. This attempt to keep your feet grounded, in a realistic view of professional expectations and boundaries, can encourage growth and create excitement about change.

This chapter will walk you through building your self-care plan for professional sustainability. These steps include (1) envisioning your path forward, (2) assessing areas of self-care, and (3) creating your professional sustainability plan. Please know this is not a one-size-fits-all approach, nor will the plan remain static for the rest of your career. The design of this is to recognize where you are today and how you can take meaningful steps toward self-care while working in higher education and hopefully create a path that makes your career in higher education a long-term possibility.

ENVISIONING YOUR PATH FORWARD

A vision for professional sustainability should serve as an inspiration for you to move forward to a more ideal future (Jordan, 2022, p. 111). We like to think of this like the portrait of that sunset we introduced in Chapter 1 of this book (Figure 10.1).

Figure 10.1. Vision for self-care and sustainability.

Source: Alexandra Laing, used with permission.

The first step is to consider what matters most to you as a professional in higher education or what type of legacy you hope to leave when you walk away from your last working day on campus. This is really charging you to consider your impact. What matters to you? What values do you want to carry through your professional life? How do you want to be remembered by your colleagues, students, or friends? Thinking about your impact should describe a thoughtful picture that explores the professional life that you desire or where you want to go and where you want to end up. You should consider what brings you the most joy in your professional life, what gives your professional life meaning, what you are most passionate about, or what you want to contribute to the field. This is how you will create your impact statement.

Through visualization, you reflect upon your own wisdom to inform your path forward. To feel like your professional life was impactful, you do need to plan—not just the day-to-day tasks but also the bigger ideas and milestones you hope to encounter during your professional journey. Think of this as a long journey—if you wander aimlessly, you may miss important milestones along the way. The more compelling impact you can create, the more likely you are to move to action to achieve that impact (Jordan, 2022, p. 207). Later in this book, we have created an open-ended response journal for you to use to brainstorm your professional impact—how you hope to be remembered, the values you hope you are remembered for, and the accomplishments you'd like to achieve as a professional in higher education. As you work through the prompts, it is okay to not have all the answers immediately. You may need some time to reflect to identify meaningful and thoughtful answers.

IMPACT STATEMENT PROMPTS

1. Who do you hope to impact during your professional journey? Be specific. Focus on who you want to inspire to move towards growth and positive results.
2. What are the aspects of higher education you hope to inspire through your journey? Be specific. Use action verbs.
3. How will you inspire this impact? What specific steps will you take now, later, and much later to build a process that is sustainable?
4. What is the purpose of your impact plan? Be specific. Try something like: The purpose of this impact plan is to (inspire, connect, build, other verb) (specific people/groups) to do (the desired behavior).

(McKenzie & Oltman, 2022)

Once you have considered what you hope your professional impact might be, begin drafting a professional impact statement—a concise, clear, and personal professional goal that captures what you hope your impact will be and how you will attempt to get there. You should write in first person and make statements about the future you desire. While each person's vision will be unique, some prompts to start the vision statement include:

- I want my professional impact to be . . .
- To achieve this impact, I will need to . . .
- I hope my impact does . . .

Provided next is space to start the process of drafting your professional vision.

Professional Impact Statement—Draft

After you complete your first draft, share it with a professional colleague you know well and trust to ask for feedback. A few prompts to guide the conversation are:

- Do you think this professional impact statement reflects who I am?
- Is there anything I should add or that I have forgotten within this statement?
- Is there anything unclear or not accurate in the statement?

Once you complete the conversation with your colleague, update your impact statement in the following form.

Professional Impact Statement

ADDING SELF-CARE TO PROFESSIONAL IMPACT AND SUSTAINABILITY

Planning for impact is one aspect of having an extensive career in higher education—the other, as we have covered throughout this book, is finding ways to manage self-care during the various challenges that the environment of colleges and universities naturally creates for its professionals. We purposefully did not design a list of top 100 self-care tactics because those tools can be quite lengthy and impersonal. As you have seen from the topics covered in this book, managing during times of change or building a meaningful plan for yourself is more than facing the need to quit smoking or taking a walk break at lunch. Don't be mistaken—we wholeheartedly encourage daily self-care practices that fit who you are and where you are in your health and wellness journey, but the self-care processes we hope you'll uncover from what you've read in this book are more global and professionally oriented. For example, what types of recognition are meaningful to you? Who can help you build a more comprehensive plan of clear communication? What do you control, and what is out of your control? Think through each of the topics covered in this book and reflect on how the exploration of each impacted your reflections about your professional sustainability.

Now that you have crafted a professional impact statement, it is time to use the content of the book chapters to guide the areas of self-care that need to be addressed to make your desired future in higher education a reality. In the scale presented next, identify from 1, being least important to 5, being most important, which areas you need to focus on for professional sustainability (see Table 10.1).

Table 10.1 Assessing Areas of Professional Self-Care

Assessing Areas of Professional Self-Care		
Rank	Areas in higher education that warrant self-care action for you	Rating Scale 1: Least important to 5: Most important
	Communication	1 2 3 4 5
	Role clarity	1 2 3 4 5
	Lack of control	1 2 3 4 5
	Meaningful recognition	1 2 3 4 5
	Confidence in leadership	1 2 3 4 5
	Delegation	1 2 3 4 5
	Professional growth	1 2 3 4 5
	Job creep and high-achieving habits	1 2 3 4 5

Source: Created by Vicki Bautista.

Using the results of the chart, rank in order from 1 to 8 in the column labeled "Rank" which professional self-care topics are most important for you to address moving forward today. Then respond to these questions:

Which professional self-care topics scored the highest? Why?

Which professional self-care topics scored the lowest? Why?

Did you rank any of your highest scored topics as your number one area to focus on? What steps can you take today to begin to implement changes in that area?

FORMALIZING YOUR SELF-CARE PLAN FOR PROFESSIONAL SUSTAINABILITY

As you reflect on the areas you want to pursue for your self-care and professional sustainability plan, you should try to understand where you are today. The reflection questions provided within each chapter, along with each chapter's activity, helped guide you to think. Using those various results and compilation of thoughts, you can begin to form your self-care and professional sustainability plan here.

Step 1: Review each chapter's activity and reflection questions. What did you learn in each chapter? What areas resonated with you and why? Where do you want to spend more time learning about a chapter topic? We pause here to ask you to consider the following questions:

- What surprised you about building an extended professional life in higher education?
- What opportunities do you see for yourself professionally within higher education?
- Where are you today compared to where you want to be professionally, at the end of your career?

Step 2: Now think about the concept of self-care within each of the topics covered in this book. As you read, what self-care topics were personally relevant to you? Now, consider each of these questions:

- Think about the current state of your self-care within your professional life. It may be well balanced, somewhat balanced, or completely unbalanced. All of us have phases of each of these, but where are you today?
- Now, consider how you envision a better self-care balance impacting your professional performance and longevity. If your self-care were routine and in focus, how do you think your professional life would change?

Step 3: Think about self-care and professional sustainability in concert—together—like a symphony of sorts. A carefully constructed maze of sounds, people, tasks, and responses. This is where you will begin to build your self-care and professional sustainability plan.

Step 4: Begin working through the self-care plan for professional sustainability provided in Appendix. This template explores the unique aspects of working in higher education as explored throughout this book. Consider your own needs, desires, and professional aspirations. Know that you will not be able to address all of these issues and challenges at once. Instead, pick the topic (or topics) that are most prominent or pressing in your life today. Consider how you can take action to create change in that one area. Begin small. Create actionable steps. Give it some time. Then stop and reassess your progress. Over time, expand your approach to include additional areas or issues that impact your self-care and professional sustainability.

A LIVING SELF-CARE AND PROFESSIONAL SUSTAINABILITY PLAN

Now that you have drafted some ideas for your self-care and professional sustainability plan, we need you to recognize that this is a living plan—that is, it is not a one-and-done approach to solving your professional issues. Rather, it is a one-page self-guided document that focuses specifically on the two areas of concern in this book: self-care and professional sustainability in higher education. After reading this book and considering the landscape of what you have seen and experienced in higher education, you have opinions, views, and a heightened awareness of these issues. You picked this book up because you knew these were areas at odds—that your professional life was causing direct conflict within your self-care aspirations. Thus, this plan should be living—it should be posted near you, reviewed often, and updated as your career develops. The one stable piece of the plan should be your professional impact statement. If done well, that will remain consistent over time and throughout the various professional roles and positions you fill throughout your career. That guiding statement should shape how you design your self-care practices and how you prioritize growth within your professional sustainability.

A CALL TO ACTION

Creating a self-care plan for professional sustainability is a highly personal process. It asks you to think about your role in higher education in a variety of ways—the tasks you do, the people you work alongside, and the responsibilities you carry. The work you do is hard, and over time, it can wear you down. In this work of reflection, thinking about the challenges and opportunities in higher education and becoming more strategic about how you can create professional sustainability for yourself, consider how you might also create change in the field itself. What is it that you can do to create better self-care conditions on your campus? How can you collaborate with others to provide a bit of space to discuss role clarity or the chaos of change? What talents can you share with those newer to higher education about how you managed when roles became fuzzy and your work–life balance was completely upended? You can create change in the ethos of your campus by leading conversations about what the institution is doing to care for its employees and how it is providing a place where professionals want to stay for the duration of their career.

SOME LAST NOTES TO THE READER

As authors, we hope that as you worked your way through the pages in this book you saw yourself. Investing in a long-term professional life in higher education is not simple, nor is it always a clear path, but the work can be rewarding and can help fill that desire to make your work mean something. We circle back to where we started our thoughts on balancing self-care and professional sustainability in higher education: the work of Professor Elizabeth Haswell, author of a 2017 article titled "Point of View: The Sustainable Professor." In that work, Haswell articulated the increasing demands on campuses today, particularly that on faculty who are tasked with teaching, service, and research as only parts of their actual jobs. Adding to these traditional assignments was the increasing demand for responsivity, administrative service, and meeting students' needs as anything from a coach, to a mental health consultant, to a career expert. The roles in higher education are getting more complex, not less.

Haswell proposed that we compare our role in higher education to agriculture—both are processes that need nurturing and protection. She suggests the essential roles we hold (for faculty, this might be teaching, research, and service) as the topsoil of our profession. This element can be easily swept aside, impacted by toxic chemicals (influences from outside), and shaped by the changing conditions. If we feed the topsoil low-nutrient conditions (for us, this would be sustaining our work life on coffee, little sleep, and ignored relationships), we lose the ability to dig deeper into that soil of our richer professional lives. Protecting that topsoil is a basic role we all need to manage to be able to make deeper and more meaningful impact—and in the end, we hope that is what we are all able to achieve.

Appendix

To create your self-care plan for professional sustainability, use this template to think through each area you've read about in this book. As you work through each section of the template, know that some of the answers may not come easily or automatically, and you may need time to reflect in order to identify the areas that you'd like to focus on within your self-care plan. Use the spaces within the template to create simple and honest responses. Do not worry about filling in all of the spaces, but rather focus on thinking about areas of self-care that are most important to your professional sustainability today.

SELF-CARE PLAN FOR PROFESSIONAL SUSTAINABILITY

Why does self-care and professional sustainability in higher education matter to me? List the top three reasons.			
1.			
2.			
3.			
Step 1	**Step 2**	**Step 3**	**Step 4**
What specific **areas** do I need to focus on? (Review the reflection questions from each chapter to help generate this list.)	What practices and/or strategies can I **implement** to better manage my self-care and professional sustainability?	How will I **assess** my growth for professional sustainably?	How often will I review my **progress** for this area of self-care and professional sustainability?

(*continued*)

SAMPLE RESPONSE: Role clarity	*Create a list of roles and responsibilities as they exist today*	*Have a conversation with my department chair to discuss responsibilities that have been added on over time.*	*Monthly; review the list of responsibilities and add and remove what has changed*

Considerations for moving forward:

- How can I use this plan to sustain my career in higher education?
- When should I review and update this plan in light of the constant change in the field and my evolution as a professional?
- Who can I share this plan with to promote support and accountability?
- Is there anyone at work or outside of work who can help support me in my efforts to build stronger self-care and professional sustainability strategies?
- How can I recognize and support others in their journey to build self-care strategies for professional sustainability in higher education?

References

Altman, M. (2021, April 13). *Meaningful recognition to celebrate nurses.* American Association of Critical-Care Nurses. https://www.aacn.org/blog/meaningful-recognition-to-celebrate-nurses

American Institute of Stress. (2025). *Workplace stress.* https://www.stress.org/workplace-stress/

Australian Council of Professions. (2025). *What is a profession?* https://professions.org.au/what-is-a-professional/

Baker, V. L. (2023, June 22). *A title does not a leader make.* Inside Higher Ed. https://www.insidehighered.com/opinion/career-advice/2023/06/22/higher-ed-needs-invest-more-developing-leaders-opinion

Bichsel, J., Fuesting, M., Tubbs, D., & Schneider, J. (2023, September). *The CUPA-HR 2023 higher education employee retention survey.* College and University Professional Association for Human Resources. https://www.cupahr.org/surveys/research-briefs/higher-ed-employee-retention-survey-findings-september-2023/

Burmicky, J., McClure, K. R., & Ryu, W. (2024). *Competencies for the college presidency: A national study of effective leadership in higher education.* Academic Search.

Cambridge Dictionary. (n.d.). Sustainability. In *Cambridge dictionary.org.* Retrieved March 2, 2025, from https://dictionary.cambridge.org/us/dictionary/english/sustainability

Chronicle of Higher Education. (2022, December 14). *"Higher Ed is a scam of a career": Readers speak out on dead end jobs.* https://www.chronicle.com/article/higher-ed-is-a-scam-of-a-career-readers-speak-out-on-dead-end-jobs

Darling-Hammond, L., Hyler, M. E., & Gardner, M. (2017). *Effective teacher professional development.* Learning Policy Institute. https://doi.org/10.54300/122.311

Davies, M. (2011). Concept mapping, mind mapping and argument mapping: What are the differences and do they matter? *Higher Education, 62,* 279–301. https://link.springer.com/article/10.1007/s10734-010-9387-6

Edwards, G. (2013, March 26). 5 reasons to consider a career in higher ed. *USA Today.* https://www.usatoday.com/story/news/nation/2013/03/26/consider-a-career-in-higher-ed/2022195/

Flaherty, C. (2022, July 4). *Calling it quits*. Inside Higher Ed. https://www.insidehighered.com/news/2022/07/05/professors-are-leaving-academe-during-great-resignation

Flynn, F. J., & Lide, C. R. (2023). Communication miscalibration: The price leaders pay for not sharing enough. *Academy of Management Journal, 66*(4), 1102–1122. https://doi.org/10.5465/amj.2021.0245

Freudenberger, H. J., & Richelson, G. (1980). *Burn-out: The high cost of achievement*. Anchor Press.

Friedman, R. (2025). *5 things high-performing teams do differently*. Ignite80. https://www.ignite80.com/insights/5-things-high-performing-teams-do-differently-by-ron-friedman-ph-d/

Fuesting, M., & Schneider, J. (2023). *The CUPA-HR 2022 higher education employee retention survey: Focus on supervisors*. CUPA-HR. https://www.cupahr.org/surveys/research-briefs/higher-ed-employee-retention-survey-focus-on-supervisors-january-2023

Gallup. (2024, June 28). *The importance of employee recognition: Low cost, high impact*. https://www.gallup.com/workplace/236441/employee-recognition-low-cost-high-impact.aspx#:~:text=Workplace%20recognition%20motivates%2C%20provides%20a,company%2C%20leading%20to%20higher%20retention

Garr, S. (2022, September 19). *Why your team members need daily check-is*. Harvard Business Review. https://hbr.org/2022/09/why-your-team-members-need-daily-check-ins

Grosskopf, H. J. (2018). *Awake leadership: A system for leading with clarity and creativity*. Awake Solutions.

Grossman, D. (2023, July 17). *6 benefits of delegation (and why most leaders underdelegate)*. The Grossman Group. https://www.yourthoughtpartner.com/blog/the-benefits-of-delegation-and-why-most-leaders-under-delegate

Haswell, E. (2017). *Point of view: The sustainable professor*. *eLife*. https://elifesciences.org/articles/31083

Healthy Minds Network. (2024). *The healthy minds study: 2023–2024 faculty and staff report*. https://healthymindsnetwork.org/wp-content/uploads/2024/10/HMS-2024-Faculty-Staff-National-Data-Report.pdf

Johnson, J. (2020). *What is decision fatigue?* Medical News Today. https://www.medicalnewstoday.com/articles/decision-fatigue

Jordan, M. (2022). *How to be a health coach: An integrative wellness approach*. Global Medicine Enterprises.

Kim, J. (2017, August 16). *The casual disparagement of higher ed staff*. Inside Higher Ed. https://www.insidehighered.com/blogs/technology-and-learning/casual-disparagement-higher-ed-staff#

King-White, D. L., & Rogers, E. E. (2018). *Promoting self-care and work-life balance among practitioners in higher education*. Adult Higher Education Alliance.

Koster, M., & McHenry, K. (2023). Areas of work-life that contribute to burnout among higher education health science faculty and perception of institutional support. *International Journal of Qualitative Studies on Health and Well-Being, 18*(1), 1–9. https://doi.org/10.1080/17482631.2023.2235129

Kreuter, N. (2014, April 20). *The difficulty of delegating.* Insider Higher Ed. https://www.insidehighered.com/advice/2014/04/21/essay-importance-academics-learning-how-delegate#)Delegation

Krishna, D. K. (2018). Decoding 7C's in effective communication. *International Journal of Communication, 28*(1–2), 37–46.

Kuncl, L., & Christiansen, K. (2024, February 1). *Overworked and undervalued: Retaining top educators.* Gallup. https://www.gallup.com/education/609422/overworked-undervalued-retaining-top-educators.aspx

Lederman, D. (2022, May 3). *Turnover, burnout, and demoralization in higher ed.* Inside Higher Ed. https://www.insidehighered.com/news/2022/05/04/turnover-burnout-and-demoralization-higher-ed

Lloyd, S. (2024, June 25). *Managers must delegate effectively to develop employees.* SHRM. https://www.shrm.org/topics-tools/news/organizational-employee-development/managers-must-delegate-effectively-to-develop-employees

Lowney, C. (2003). *Heroic leadership: Best practices from a 450-year old company that changed the world.* Loyola Press.

Martínez, N., Connelly, C. D., Pérez, A., & Calero, P. (2021). Self-care: A concept analysis. *International Journal of Nursing Sciences, 8*(4), 418–425. https://doi.org/10.1016/j.ijnss.2021.08.007

Mayo Clinic. (2023). *Job burnout: How to spot it and take action.* https://www.mayoclinic.org/healthy-lifestyle/adult-health/in-depth/burnout/art-20046642

McKenzie, W., & Oltman, G. (2022). Impact planning for educators [Conference Presentation], ASCD Annual Conference, Denver, CO.

Melidona, D., Cecil, B. G., Cassell, A., & Chessman, H. M. (2023). *The American college president: 2023 edition—executive summary.* American Council on Education. https://www.acenet.edu/Documents/American-College-President-2023-Exec-Summary.pdf

Meyer, T. (2023, October 19). *How to encourage employees to pursue professional development.* Business News Daily. https://www.businessnewsdaily.com/10092-encourage-professional-development.html

Middlehurst, R. (2009). Developing higher education professionals: Challenges and possibilities. In G. Gordon & C. Whitchurch (Eds.), *Academic and professional identities in higher education: The challenges of a diversifying workforce* (International Studies in Higher Education) (pp. 223–244). Routledge.

Miller, J. J., Grise-Owens, E., & Shalash, N. (2018). Investigating the self-care practices of social work faculty: An exploratory study. *Social Work Education, 37*(8), 1044–1059.

Mittelmeier, J. (2023, March 31). *The glorification of overwork in academia and its impact on our collective wellbeing.* Voices of Academia. https://voicesofacademia.com/2023/03/31/the-glorification-of-overwork-in-academia-and-its-impacts-on-our-collective-wellbeing-by-jenna-mittelmeier/

Moody, J. (2024, September 16). *Study: The 7 competencies presidents need.* Inside Higher Ed. https://www.insidehighered.com/news/governance/executive-leadership/2024/09/16/study-seven-competencies-presidents-need

Mudrak, J., Zabrodska, K., Kveton, P., Jelinek, M., Blatny, M., Solcova, I., & Machovcova, K. (2018). Occupational well-being among university faculty: A job demands-resources model. *Research in Higher Education, 59,* 325–348.

Nadler, D. P., Lu, M., & Miller, M. T. (2017, Fall). Power of the faculty: Consequences of no confidence votes on college presidents. *Journal of Research on the College President, 1*(1), 5.

Nietzel, M. T. (2023, September 23). *Why so many university presidents are facing no-confidence votes.* Forbes. https://www.forbes.com/sites/michaeltnietzel/2023/09/23/why-so-many-university-presidents-are-facing-no-confidence-votes/

NIRSA: Leaders in Collegiate Recreation, NASPA—Student Affairs Administrators in Higher Education & ACHA—American College Health Association. (2020, November). Inter-association definition of well-being. www.nirsa.org/hands-in

Progressive Mastery Learning. (2025). *Task-mastery checklist* (download). https://www.teachbetter.com/wp-content/uploads/2020/11/Task-Delegation-Worksheet-Free-Download.pdf

Riegel, D. L. (2019, June 24). *The assumptions employees make when they don't get feedback.* Harvard Business Review. https://hbr.org/2019/06/the-assumptions-employees-make-when-they-dont-get-feedback

Ryder, G. (2021). *Lips, eyes, and all that: Reading and understanding body language.* PsychCentral. https://psychcentral.com/health/body-language#understanding-and-reading-it

Sarasa, A. (2025, March 12). *Demoralization: Definition and examples in the workplace.* Meditopia. https://meditopia.com/en/forwork/articles/demoralization

Schaffner, A. K. (2023, June 1). *Understanding the circles of control, influence & concern.* https://positivepsychology.com/circles-of-influence/

Van Dyne, L. I. N. N., & Ellis, J. B. (2004). Job creep: A reactance theory perspective on organizational citizenship behavior as over-fulfillment of obligations. In L. E. Tetrick, L. M. Shore, & J. A. Coyle-Shapiro (Eds.), *The employment relationship: Examining psychological and contextual perspectives* (pp. 181–205). Oxford University Press.

Wansink, B., & Sobal, J. (2007). Mindless eating: The 200 daily food decisions we overlook. *Environment and Behavior, 39*(1), 106–123.

Wigert, B., & Tatel, C. (2024, December 3). *The great detachment: Why employees feel stuck.* Gallup. https://www.gallup.com/workplace/653711/great-detachment-why-employees-feel-stuck.aspx

World Health Organization. (2019, May 28). Burn-out an "occupational phenomenon": International Classification of Diseases. https://www.who.int

/news/item/28-05-2019-burn-out-an-occupational-phenomenon-international-classification-of-diseases

World Health Organization. (2023, February 21). Stress. https://www.who.int/news-room/questions-and-answers/item/stress

Zak, P. (2017). *The neuroscience of trust.* Harvard Business Review. https://hbr.org/2017/01/the-neuroscience-of-trust

Index

About the Authors

Gretchen Oltman is an associate professor of interdisciplinary studies at Creighton University in Omaha, Nebraska. She serves as the program director for a master's degree program in organizational leadership. Oltman is a licensed attorney and holds a PhD in educational administration. Her work spans over two decades in education, from serving as a secondary classroom instructor to leading in an administrative capacity at the university level. She is the author or coauthor of eight books written for educators and leaders, including *Building and Leading New Academic Programs in Higher Education: A Practical Guide for Faculty, What's Your Leadership Story?: A School Leader's Guide to Aligning How You Lead with Who You Are, Law Meets Literature: A Novel Approach for the English Classroom,* and *Violence in Student Writing: A School Administrator's Guide.*

Vicki Bautista, NBC-HWC, currently serves as the Doctor of Education program director at Clarkson College. She has 15 years of diverse experience in higher education, during which she has held multiple roles and responsibilities such as course instructor, program administrator, instructional designer, curriculum developer, and faculty development coordinator. She is also a board-certified health and wellness coach through the National Board for Health and Wellness Coaching. Prior to her career in higher education, she worked in health promotion and wellness across nonprofit, government, and health care sectors. She has spoken at local and national events on topics related to leadership and well-being, addressing a variety of audiences, including higher education administrators, health care providers, K–12 educational leaders, and nonprofit executives.

About the Authors